The Girl's Guide to Home Skills

Published by
THE HOMEMAKER'S MENTOR

Compiled by:

Martha Greene ❧ Jan Drexler ❧ Rebekah Wilson

"This is what every girl ought to know, for all of you expect when you grow up to have a nice home of your own, and wouldn't it be simply dreadful if you didn't know how to take care of it properly?"

from <u>Housekeeping, Cookery, Sewing for Little Girls</u> by Olive Hyde Foster circa ❖ 1922

THE GIRL'S GUIDE
TO HOME SKILLS

Published by
The Homemaker's Mentor.com
PO Box 1187
Canmer, KY 42722

PRINTED IN THE USA

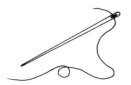

BONUS DOWNLOADABLE RESOURCES!

You may download
PRINTABLE COPIES of
selected checklists, charts, patterns,
and bonus project pages from this book
(for your personal use only)
at

TheHomemakersMentor.com/GirlsGuideExtras

My Dear Girls ~

You are embarking on a most wonderful and honorable quest: to learn how to keep a home for your family! What you will learn in the following pages will be of such help to your MotherDear now as you are a daughter in your family's home. In the future, the lessons learned will be invaluable to you when you are a young wife and the keeper of your own home.

Within these pages you will learn that there are three major elements to home skills. The first is to have a plan. Without a plan in mind when you start a task, you will never be able to finish it successfully. The second is to know which tools to use for each task, and to have them on hand. The third is routine. Once you have a routine in place, each task then has its appointed time. You'll find this and much more in this complete guide for girls that I have to share with you. I'd encourage you to always be ready to learn from MotherDear as you work by her side and enjoy all the bits of wisdom found tucked in the pages from Grandmother Foster.

Keeping a home is not a difficult thing to learn, but is a necessary part of a happy home life. As you learn to keep your home clean, to order your tasks well, and to economize both your money and your time, you will be learning the skills you need to take your place as a young woman at home. I hope "Home" will be where your heart is. . .

- Aunt Sophie

A Girl's Guide to Home Skills

Each section of this guide will take you through the areas of a home giving you checklists, scheduling charts, along with detailed instructions to learn the necessary skills for housekeeping and making it home-sweet-home.

Sparkling Clean Bathrooms

A Guide to
Cleaning & Maintaining Bathrooms
in the Home

My dear girls ~

The bathroom may not be the best loved room in the home, or the one you want to clean first, but it is certainly the most used room in the house!

One of our goals as homemakers is to keep each room in the house clean, orderly and inviting. It isn't hard to do this in the bathroom, but it takes consistent attention.

On the next page you will find a checklist of home skills you can learn to do well and become a capable keeper of a home. As you become confident through practice of these skills, MotherDear can sign the checklist to show your accomplishments.

I hope you will learn to love having a clean bathroom as much as I do!

- Aunt Sophie

Sparkling Clean Bathrooms
Home Skills List

"It is well for you to notice the way your mother does, and learn the reason she has for her method."

I can confidently do a good and thorough job in a bathroom by knowing the skills needed in the home regarding:

___ How to clean a sink
___ How to unclog a drain
___ How to clean a tub or shower stall
___ How to clean a toilet
___ How to clean the flooring in the bathroom
___ How to make bathroom mirrors clean and sparkling
___ How to fold towels and washcloths
___ How to properly care for the trash & trash containers
___ Supplies needed for the bathrooms
___ Proper hygiene
___ Bathroom etiquette
___ Procedure for an overflowing or clogged toilet
___ Procedure for the emergency of broken water pipes

NAME: _____
has passed the requirements for our home listed above and has proven herself a capable keeper of a home.

Signed:

- *MotherDear*

Getting Started

I'm sure most of you have faced a dirty bathroom with a helpless feeling. Sometimes trying to decide just where to start first can be overwhelming! There are many details involved in a bathroom, and it must be kept not just neat, but clean – germs and soap scum aren't allowed!

Here is Aunt Sophie's scheduling chart for a bathroom. Notice that the daily tasks are quite easy and can be done in just a few minutes. And if the daily tasks are kept up, then the weekly ones become much easier. Make these tasks part of your daily, weekly and monthly routines, and you'll find that you'll never again have to face a dirty bathroom!

Make a copy of this checklist for each bathroom in your house, and tape it to the inside of one of the cupboard doors. Refer to it often as you develop the habit of keeping your bathrooms clean.

Sparkling Clean Bathrooms
Scheduling Chart

DAILY

- Check toilet and wipe down lid and rim with disinfectant
- Take any soiled towels, or dirty clothes to the laundry area
- Wipe sink surface countertop
- Check trashcan

WEEKLY

- Clean toilet thoroughly
- Clean tub and shower
- Clean sink and countertop
- Clean mirror
- Clean toothbrush holder
- Sweep and mop floor
- Empty trash and replace liner

MONTHLY

- Clean out bathroom cupboards and tidy up shelves
- Dust corners and ceilings
- Wipe down cupboard doors & shelves
- Wash shower curtain if needed
- Clean drains with soda and vinegar

SEASONALLY

Restock cupboards with needed toiletries and supplies
Add a pretty new touch to the room or a fresh coat of paint

Skills for Daily Cleaning

It is helpful to have the cleaners and supplies you use daily stored in each bathroom. A small container, such as a plastic bucket, can hold rags and a spray bottle of cleaner and will fit easily under the sink or in another out of the way place. If there is no place in your bathroom, then find a place somewhere nearby where it will be handy.

There are four items on Aunt Sophie's daily chart:

- **Check toilet and wipe down lid and rim with disinfectant**
- **Take any soiled towels or dirty clothes to the laundry area**
- **Wipe sink and countertop**
- **Check trashcan**

Check toilet and wipe down lid and rim with disinfectant:

The toilet can easily be the grimiest spot in the whole house, and the least appetizing to clean. But those facts also make it one of the most **important** places to clean daily. This is where paper towels come in handy, but you can also use a supply of small towels or old washcloths that you replace daily.

First, spray some disinfectant or all-purpose cleaner on your towel. Then wipe the toilet tank, the cover, the bottom of the cover, the seat, the bottom of the seat, the toilet rim, the outside of the toilet bowl and the floor around it. Aunt Sophie works in this order so that she is cleaning from the least to most dirty areas.

Now take the toilet brush and swish around the inside of the toilet bowl along the water line and under the rim of the toilet. Rinse the brush, flush the toilet, and place the handle of the brush on the rim of the toilet with the wet brush dangling over the water. Place the toilet seat down to hold the brush in place. This will let it air dry. Ask the next person using the bathroom to put the brush away.

Take any soiled towels or dirty clothes to the laundry area:

Replace the hand towel with a clean one, straighten any other towels that are hanging crookedly, and pick up any clothes that might be on the floor.

Wipe sink and countertop:

Clean off the countertop next to the sink, and spray the sink, faucets and countertop with disinfectant or all-purpose spray cleaner. Using a clean rag or paper towel wipe down all of the surfaces, leaving them clean and shiny. If you want the faucets to be extra nice, use glass cleaner when you wipe them.

Check trashcan:

Empty the trashcan and replace the liner if it is your regular trash day. Otherwise, check it to make sure it isn't smelly or too full. If it is, go ahead and empty it.

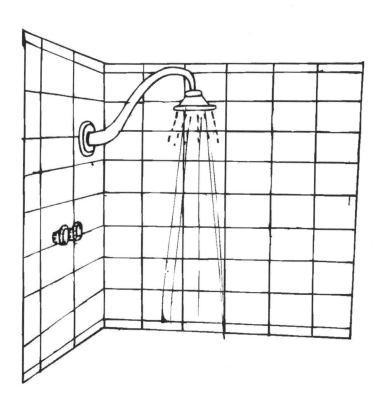

Skills for Weekly Cleaning

Since Aunt Sophie keeps up with her daily cleaning, the weekly cleaning in the bathroom is a breeze. It takes a bit longer than the daily cleaning because there are more tasks, but you won't be facing a dirty, grimy mountain of cleaning! Before starting, it's a good idea to open the bathroom window and prop open the door to get the best ventilation that you can. It will help keep you from breathing too many chemical fumes and freshen up the air in the bathroom. Even in the coldest weather Aunt Sophie will open the window an inch or so to get some fresh air into this small room!

Here are the items in Aunt Sophie's chart for weekly cleaning:

- **Clean toilet thoroughly**
- **Clean tub and shower**
- **Clean sink and countertop**
- **Clean mirror & toothbrush holder**
- **Put our fresh towels and washcloths**
- **Sweep and mop floor**
- **Empty trash and replace liner**

Clean Toilet Thoroughly:

Clean the toilet the same way you do every day, but this time when you swish the bowl with your brush, add about ½ cup of white vinegar to the water or use a commercial toilet bowl cleanser. Scrub thoroughly with your brush making sure you reach under the rim, and pay special attention to the water line. Rinse off your brush completely in running water – you can do it by flushing the toilet and holding the brush in the swirling water – and let the brush dry as usual.

Clean Tub and Shower:

Spray the walls of your tub or shower with your cleaning agent. You'll want one that dissolves soap scum, or use the homemade soap scum remover or the homemade basic all-purpose cleaner. After spraying the shower walls, let the cleaner sit for a few minutes to soften up the dirt. While you're waiting, use your time well! This is a good time to take the rug outside to shake it, or remove items from the counter next to the sink.

Next take a rag, sponge or soft brush to scrub the walls. What you choose to use depends on what your tub or shower walls are made of.

> **For fiberglass:** use a sponge, rag or soft cloth.

> **For tile or porcelain:** use a sponge, rag or soft plastic bristled brush

> **For plastic surfaces:** use a plastic bristled brush

Aunt Sophie never forgets to wipe the top edge of the shower or tub surround, as that is a place we seldom see, but where dust collects. If you have a shower door, be sure to wipe the tracks for a sliding door, or the frame of a swinging door.

After scrubbing the walls of your shower, fill a large plastic cup with clean water and pour it carefully down the walls to rinse them. Now that the walls are rinsed you can let them air dry, or you can wipe the walls with a clean towel to dry them.

Next, spray the sides and bottom of your tub or the floor of your shower with your cleaner. Scrub with your sponge, rag or soft plastic bristled brush like you did on the walls. You may run into stubborn bathtub rings or dirt on the floor on your shower, and be sure to scrub those with your cleansing powder or gel. Rinse, using your plastic cup.

Clean Sink and Countertop:

Remove everything from the countertop so you are able to clean it thoroughly. Spray the counter with an all-purpose or disinfecting cleaner and wipe it down. Then use a cleansing powder or gel to clean the sink. Rinse both areas thoroughly.

Clean Mirror and Toothbrush Holder:

Remove the toothbrushes from the toothbrush holder and clean it with soap and water or with your disinfecting cleaner. Rinse it well, dry it, and replace the toothbrushes.

For the mirror, spray it with glass cleaner and wipe it well with an old, crumpled newspaper. Be sure to wipe it thoroughly so that you don't leave any streaks. Before you leave this area, spray the sink and faucets with the glass cleaner and wipe them with a soft cloth. It will really make your sink shine!

Put Out Fresh Towels and Washcloths:

Replace all of the towels on the towel racks. Take pride in how you place the towels on the racks!

Ask yourself:

Are they hanging neatly with the edges even?
Are the colors pleasing together?
Are there enough towels and washcloths for everyone who uses this bathroom?

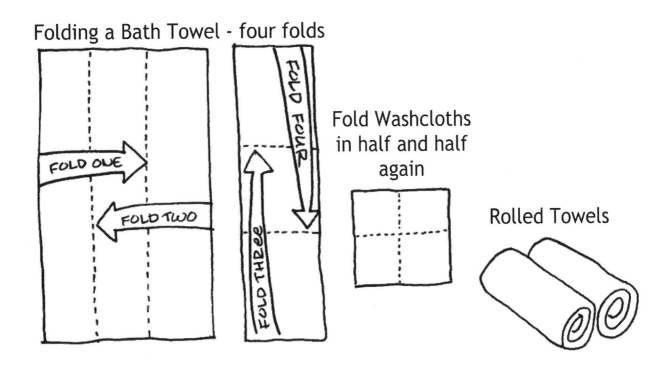

Folding a Bath Towel - four folds

FOLD ONE

FOLD TWO

FOLD FOUR

FOLD THREE

Fold Washcloths in half and half again

Rolled Towels

Towel tip:
It also works very nicely in some storage areas for a convenient fit and for a tidy appearance, to roll towels and washcloths. Use towel fold 1 & 2, then roll up tightly and stack towel rolls: 3 on the bottom, 2 on the next row and then 1 on top. Fold washcloths only once and then roll. These fit nicely in small baskets kept handy near sinks and tubs.

Sweep and Mop Floor:

First, take out the rugs and shake them if you didn't do this earlier. Then sweep the floor. Aunt Sophie's favorite way to sweep a bathroom floor is to use the hose attachment on her vacuum cleaner because it can reach into all of the small spaces, but you can also use a broom and dust pan. Once the floor is swept, then it's time to mop it.

You can mop the floor using plain water or a floor cleaner. Aunt Sophie likes to spray the floor around the toilet with the disinfecting or all-purpose cleaner before mopping. Be careful not to just move dirt around while you mop! You don't want to have a ring of dirt around the edges of the room when you're finished cleaning. Rinse your mop often, and be sure to clean along the edges and floorboards as you go.

Replace the rugs after the floor is dry.

Empty Trash and Replace Liner:

This is the time when you go ahead and empty the trash whether you think it needs it or not. You want to leave the whole bathroom fresh and clean!

Before you leave the bathroom, Aunt Sophie takes a last look.

Does it look clean, fresh and inviting?

Spritz the room with a scented air freshener if you like, close the window if needed, and you're done!

Caring for the Trash Container

To prevent a build up of dust, grime and bacteria the trash container should be cleaned out every month at least.

To clean the trash can, remove the trash bag and tie closed. Set aside.

Place the trash can under the bathtub facet and fill 1/4 full with hot water. Add a few tablespoons of laundry detergent and allow to dissolve by swishing the water and detergent around in the trash can. Once dissolved, use a scrub brush to clean the inside and outside of the trash can. If there was a strong odor in the trash can, allow to soak with the detergent water for 30 minutes before emptying in bathtub and rinsing well. Dry completely.

Place an empty, folded trash bag in the bottom of the trash can and then place a trash bag into the trash can, open and ready to be used. In a pinch, you can quickly exchange the used bag for the new if visitors are arriving. This extra bag also can help make easier clean up for next time.

Aunt Sophie has used another little trick you may try: Lay a paper towel folded to fit the bottom of your can as a liner to the container and then sprinkle it liberally with baking soda. The baking soda absorbs odors and small amounts of liquid and the next time you clean the can just discard the paper liner and wash the container as directed above.

Skills for Monthly Cleaning

There are some things that need to be cleaned regularly, but not as often as your weekly tasks. These are the things that take much longer than a week to start getting dirty or out of order, but you certainly don't want them to get to the point of actually being dirty.

Here are the things on Aunt Sophie's Monthly Checklist:

- **Clean out bathroom cupboards and tidy up shelves**
- **Dust corners and ceilings**
- **Wipe down cupboard doors and other surfaces**
- **Wash shower curtain (if you have one)**
- **Clean drains**

Clean out bathroom cupboards and tidy up shelves:

This could be a big job or a small one depending on how much storage space you have in your bathroom. Your bathroom could have a lot of storage space – a linen closet and drawers as well as a cupboard or two under the sink – or it could have very little. For your monthly tasks it's important to clean the cupboards and drawers where you store toiletries, paper products and cleaning supplies. Do one shelf or drawer at a time.

First, take everything out of the drawer or off the shelf. Using your all purpose cleaner, wipe out the inside of the drawer or shelf. As you replace the items, discard anything that might be old or broken, or find another place for anything that doesn't belong there. Be sure to put the items back neatly, so that everyone in your family can find what they're looking for.

Aunt Sophie likes to use small baskets or boxes to hold some of the smaller things. Pretty baskets with items together and tidy will bring a smile to your face when you open the cupboard door!

Dust Corners and Ceilings:

This is a fun task! Take your broom and wrap a clean cloth around the bristle end of it. Aunt Sophie uses an old towel and fastens it with a safety pin to hold it on. Now gently sweep along the corners of the room where the walls meet the ceiling and where they meet each other. Your cloth will pick up any dust or cobwebs before you can even see them!

Wipe Down Cupboard Doors and Other Surfaces:

Using a cloth and a spray bottle of all-purpose cleaner, spray the outside of your cupboard doors then wipe. Try to get all of the surfaces you can reach. Aunt Sophie always wipes the light switch cover while doing this task, and don't forget the walls that are easily splashed next to the sink and toilet. Start at the door of your bathroom and work your way around the room, wiping anything that might gather dust and dirt.

Wash Shower Curtain:

Not every shower has a curtain. Yours may have a shower door that you wash weekly when you clean your shower. To wash your shower curtain take it down from the rings or hooks and put it in your washing machine. Wash it with a little laundry soap. If mildew is a problem you can add bleach or vinegar to the rinse. After the washer is finished, hang the curtain back up to dry.

Clean Drains:

Pour several big spoonfuls of baking soda into the drains of your bathtub and your sink. Pour white vinegar into the drain until you see it begin to foam. Allow it to sit for 20-30 minutes, and then run clean water down the drain. This removes the built-up scum in your pipes and deodorizes it also. Aunt Sophie does this for each of her drains every month to keep them draining well and smelling sweet.

Skills for Seasonal Cleaning

Seasonal tasks for the bathroom can be simple or more thorough: every three months, while doing monthly cleaning, she makes sure that all the bathroom supplies are stocked. Are there rolls of toilet paper that are easily accessible? Are there new bars of soap, tubes of toothpaste, and bottles of shampoo to replace ones that will be used up in the next few months? Aunt Sophie keeps all these supplies on a shelf in the bathroom so that whenever anyone needs something, it's right there.

Each season attempt to add a new touch to the room to beautify or brighten it up - like a new candle or some new hand towels? Possibly it is time for a fresh coat of paint to the walls in a new color?

Bathroom Supply List

Shampoo
Bar Soap
Liquid Soap
Washcloths
Bath Towels
Hand Towels
Air Freshener
Baking Soda
Toothpaste
Toothbrushes
Mouthwash
Dental Floss
Pumice Stone
Toilet Brush
First Aid Kit
Sponges
Scrub Brushes
Mop
Broom
Cleaning Rags

Paper Towels
Cotton Tips
Cotton Balls
Deodorant
Small Cups
Disinfectant Cleaners
Razors
Combs
Brushes
Talcum powder
Lotions
Toilet Tissue
Kleenex
Trash bags
Plunger
Small Scissors
Peroxide
Rubbing Alcohol
Facial Cosmetics

A Lesson on Bathroom Cleaners

I hope you remember that one of the three elements to successful homemaking is to have the proper tools and know how to use them. In the bathroom Aunt Sophie's most valuable tools are the cleaners used to get rid of the grime and germs that like to live in this well-used room. It is important to know what cleaners you need and what you can expect them to do. You can either buy chemical or *green* eco-friendly cleaners at the store, or you can make your own cleaners using the recipes found at the end of this section. Both work well, and making your own cleaners can help save on the household budget.

Here are the types of cleaners you will need to clean your bathroom:

Soap scum remover—removes build-up soap scum that has dried on the shower or tub walls and floor.

Glass cleaner—used for washing mirrors, windows, glass shower doors and to make chrome sparkle.

Drain cleaner—removes build-up gunk and deodorizes the bathroom drains.

Cleansing powder or gel—used to scrub smooth surfaces to remove built-up grime.

Mineral deposit remover—removes built-up mineral deposits without scratching.

Basic disinfectant—kills bacteria, viruses, mold, and mildew.

Mold and mildew remover—kills and helps dissolve mold and mildew.

Basic bathroom or All-Purpose cleaner—basic cleaning agent that can be used on any surface.

Toilet cleaner—cleans, disinfects, and some remove mineral build-up.

Tile Cleaner—used specifically on tiles to remove build-up and polish the tile.

Air freshener—used to remove airborne odors and leave the bathroom smelling fresh.

With this list of cleaning agents, you can clean any bathroom and leave it fresh, sparkling and sanitized with a minimum of effort and time. Knowing how best to use the products depends on which form you will use: chemical, _green_ eco-friendly, or homemade. For chemical cleaning agents, follow the directions on the container or bottle for best results.

NEVER mix chemical agents as toxic, even deadly, fumes can occur. Always read the directions before using a chemical agent.

Some cleaning agents need to be sprayed on and left to set for minutes or even hours for the best results. Others may need to be diluted or can not be used on specific surfaces such as fiberglass or plastic.

Green cleaning agents are health-friendly and easy to use. You should read the directions prior to using to make sure you are aware of anything unusual regarding the product. Green cleaning agents do not offer as wide a selection so you may need to incorporate homemade agents as well. The two work well together and most homemade cleaning agents are eco-friendly anyway

IMPORTANT!

Homemade cleaning agents, unless made with bleach or ammonia, can be used without too much worry and can be used in combination if necessary. But ALWAYS remember to NEVER mix bleach or ammonia together as a chlorine gas is formed when the two are mixed. The gas can be deadly if inhaled or can cause damage from the fumes burning the lining of the lungs, throat and nose. Decide whether to use bleach or ammonia in your home: only one—not both. This prevents any possibility of the two connecting. Bleach works well with disinfecting and whitening; ammonia works well with disinfecting and leaving a streak-free surface (which is why it is often used in glass cleaning products).

You can replace the ammonia with rubbing alcohol (isopropyl alcohol) for the same streak-free affect without the worry of a chemical reaction from the bleach.

Recipes for Homemade Cleaners

HomeMade Drain Cleaner

Place several big spoonfuls of baking soda into the drain to be cleaned. Pour white vinegar into the drain until you see foaming action begin. Allow this to sit undisturbed for 20-30 minutes and flush the drain with tap water. This not only removes built-up scum without damaging your pipes, but it deodorizes the drain and pipes as well.

If you do not see clearly that the drain is free and clear of debris and build up—possibly still clogged—use a long pair of tweezers or a small length of sturdy wire to poke around and try to lift out anything that could be clogging the drain. Then repeat the homemade drain cleaner and unless there is a major clog farther down in the bend of the pipes you should have a clear, free flowing access through your pipes.

If your drain still isn't open, block the overflow hole in your sink with a wet cloth. Remove the drain stopper (some unscrew, with some you need to push in, turn and pull out), then use a plunger to loosen the clog. Make sure there is some water standing in the sink, and keep plunging until the drain runs clear.

Squeaky Shine Glass Cleaner

In a clean spray bottle, mix 1 cup rubbing alcohol (isopropyl alcohol) with 2-3 cups water. Spray in a light mist over mirror and wipe dry and streak-free with old newspapers. Be sure not to use your father's current paper that arrived today, make sure it is "old news".

Simple Cleansing Powder

The easiest of all – just place baking soda into an empty, clean parmesan cheese container. Sprinkle on the area you are cleaning, and scrub with a wet rag or sponge. If you are dealing with a stubborn stain, add a little white vinegar to the baking soda after you've sprinkled it onto your surface, and watch the little bubbles scrub the dirt away.

Soap Scum Remover

Using a 32 oz. squirt bottle, place ¼ cup powdered or liquid laundry detergent into the bottle using a funnel. Pour in VERY hot water (not hot enough to melt the plastic!) until filled half full. Swish around until the detergent is completely dissolved in the water. If there are any chunks it will plug your spray nozzle. Spray the walls of your shower or sides of your tub, scrub with a wet rag or sponge, then rinse. Always use caution w/ HOT water!

Basic All-Purpose Cleaner

Mix together 2 Tablespoons baking soda and ¼ cup white vinegar. Add 2 quarts warm water. Put in a clean, empty spray bottle and use as needed. This cleaner can be used on everything from the tub to the sink to the toilet surfaces.

HomeMade Freshener for Towels

Mix 1 cup liquid fabric softener with 3 cups water. Place in a clean spray bottle and use as desired. Sprayed lightly on folded towels with freshen them up with a nice scent. This also can be used to lightly freshen the room's air. NOTE: Never try to use a freshener to cover up odors caused by dirt and such. Keep a clean and tidy bathroom!

Cleaning Tools & Supplies

Before starting to clean the bathroom, make sure you have these supplies handy:

Broom, dust pan, mop and bucket - *to use in cleaning the floor, ceiling and walls.*

Trash bags – *to refill the bathroom trash can.*

Scrubbing brushes – *I like to use an old toothbrush for small corners, and a larger one for stubborn dirt.*

Cleaning rags or sponges – *rags are easier to wash and keep clean, since bacteria grow quickly! Be sure to have separate rags for the toilet area. Paper towels come in handy for the really dirty jobs and can be disposed of quickly for big messies.*

Pumice stone – *used in removing mineral deposits.*

Rubber gloves – *either disposable or reusable. Gloves are important as you handle chemicals or clean very dirty areas.*

Small bucket – *useful for adding water to concentrated cleaning solutions. You can also use it between cleanings to store your other tools.*

Large plastic cup – *to rinse shower and tub walls.*

One More Thing

Aunt Sophie has mentioned "mineral deposits" a couple times already, and she wants to make sure you know what they are.

Some areas of the country have what is called "hard water", meaning that the water has many dissolved minerals in it. This gives each part of the country a distinctive taste to the water, but if the water is very hard, it can also leave mineral deposits on sinks and tubs. They usually form where the water drips out of a faucet. When the water dries, it leaves traces of minerals behind. These deposits can build up over time, but regular cleaning will help keep them at bay. Whether they are a problem in your bathroom or not depends on the water where you live.

Unexpected Company

There are old-fashioned sayings you may have heard from Grandmother like:

"She won't hit a lick at a snake"
(meaning: she won't do her duties but shirks them)
or
"Just give it a lick and a promise"
(meaning: quickly tidy something up and promise to come back and do a thorough cleaning at your earliest opportunity)

So if unexpected visitors suddenly arrive, this is the minimum needed to freshen the bathroom and have it ready if needed.

Remember—keeping extra supplies, including extra clean towels in the bathroom makes this job quick! Here is how to give it "A lick & A promise" . . . .

Place fresh towels out.

♥

Wipe down the toilet seat, rim of toilet and where the seat is bolted to the toilet.

♥

Check toilet paper supply and soap.

♥

Clean mirror if it is spotted or streaked.

♥

Spritz the room with air freshener.
♥

EMERGENCY! *What's a Girl to Do?*

Sometimes emergencies happen in the bathroom, and you need to know how to handle them! The most common occurrence is a toilet that is overflowing. When you press down the handle to flush the toilet and water starts filling the bowl instead of going down, don't panic! The most common reaction, and the worst one, is to try to flush the toilet again, hoping that a second flush will get rid of whatever is clogging the drain – but don't do that! It will just send more water into an already flooded bowl.

• First, if water is running out of the bowl and onto the floor, that is a real emergency and has to be taken care of right away. Grab several old towels (It is a good idea to have some of these in the bathroom just for times like this as they happen to everyone one time or another) and mop up the water as soon as possible.

• Once the flood is under control you can address the clogged toilet. Most of the time the clog is caused by too much toilet paper and other waste, but sometimes it can be caused by a foreign object dropping into the bowl. Either way, the procedure is the same.

• Keep a plunger, or "plumber's helper" handy for each bathroom. This is a rubber or plastic cone shape on the end of a handle. When used properly, it forces air into the drain when you push it in and causes suction when you pull it up. This two way action loosens the clog.

• Place the cone over the hole in the middle of the toilet bowl and methodically push on it to force air and water into the drain. Repeat this action several times.

• As the clog loosens, you will see the water level in the toilet bowl going down. At this point you can push the plunger up and down a little faster until the clog is completely cleared.

• Flush the toilet again, rinse the plunger in the clear water in the bowl, and take the towels to the laundry. Your job is done!

• If the clog isn't removed by using the plunger, you may need to use a "snake". This is a long, flexible tool that goes into the drain and pushes the clog through. This is usually a bigger job for the Mr.Fix-It of your home. Aunt Sophie's advice is to keep the toilet flushing properly is to prevent clogs in the first place. Keep the toilet lid closed between uses to prevent foreign objects from falling into it. If the overflows are caused mainly by waste, ask each family member to make sure the toilet flushes completely before they leave the bathroom.

Peek Inside the Tank

Here is a diagram showing the inside of a modern toilet tank. These tanks located behind the toilet are filled with water that makes the modern convenience of automatic flushing possible. If you actually peek inside, you'll find a maze of interesting workings as the sketch below indicates, even though it is not completely detailed. Occasionally some parts wear out and can be replaced to have the toilet working again as good as new.

In emergencies where the water is not running to the home, the tank can be manually filled with water from a bucket, and then flushed as usual.

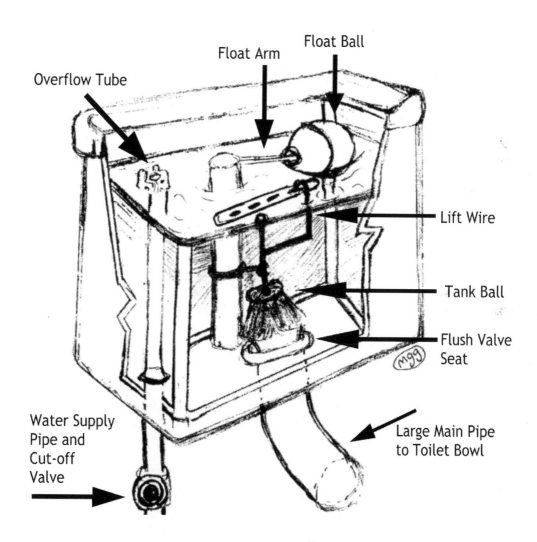

Float Ball

Float Arm

Overflow Tube

Lift Wire

Tank Ball

Flush Valve Seat

Water Supply Pipe and Cut-off Valve

Large Main Pipe to Toilet Bowl

HELP! *The Water Pipes are Leaking!*

If you have pipes that are leaking, or a mysterious puddle of water appears inside your bathroom cabinet or on the floor, it is wise to take steps immediately to stop the problem before it gets worse. MotherDear will not always be at hand so be prepared by knowing what should be done and you will be glad you prepared ahead of time for such time as this.

The first step is to find the source of the leak. There are a few possibilities to look for:

• A faucet may be leaking – you can usually identify this by the dripping that continues out of a faucet even when it is turned off all the way.

• The connection between two pipes may be loose or corroded – this kind of leak may go on for several days before you find it, since pipes are usually hidden inside cupboards and under sinks.

• The supply pipe for your toilet, or the toilet tank itself may be leaking – you can tell this if the water is mainly on the floor behind the toilet.

The next step is to stop the leak by turning off the water supply.

• Faucets usually have shut off valves underneath the sink.

• The supply pipe for your toilet also often has its own shut off valve.

• If you can't find a shut off valve, or if the leak is in the pipes themselves, then you will need to find the main shut off valve for your house's water supply.

• If you live in town, your house will probably have a valve in the basement that shuts off the supply from the city water. It often looks like a faucet on a pipe coming through the basement wall. Closing this valve will turn off the water to your whole house.

• If you don't have a shut off valve on the lower level of the home, you may need to turn off the water at the water meter during an emergency. If the water meter isn't inside your house, it may be in the yard with a metal cover over it, like a manhole cover. The valve probably needs a special tool to turn it off.

• If you have a well, find out how to turn off the water coming into your house.

Above all, be sure you know how to turn off your water before an emergency occurs!

Once you have identified the source of the problem and stopped more water from leaking, then it is time to repair the leak. Aunt Sophie reminds you that you should be quick to ask for help – your father may be able to manage the repairs, or perhaps an uncle or neighbor does well with simple plumbing repairs and will be summoned. If there is no other help available, or if the problem is a large one, a plumber may need to do the repairs.

Considering Others

Since we share the bathroom with other members of our family and with guests who come to our home, it's important to use proper etiquette in the bathroom. Here are Aunt Sophie's rules for good bathroom manners:

After using the bathroom, do a quick wipe down of the sink, counter top and toilet to clean up any splashes of water.

♥

If you empty a roll of toilet paper, replace it.

♥

After taking a shower or bath, put any toiletries you got out away and hang your towel on the towel rack neatly.

♥

While you're in the bathroom, have consideration that others may be waiting to use the facilities, especially if your home only has one bathroom.

Aunt Sophie would like to remind you that one way discord can make its way into a family is for family members to complain about each other – and the bathroom is a common place for complaints! If the person before you didn't use consideration, don't complain about it. Use this opportunity to serve your family! Go ahead and replace the toilet paper, or wipe down the counter. If it is something that occurs often, you can bring it to MotherDear's attention privately – but don't make an issue of it.

Bible Memory Verses for the Family

"Be ye kind one to another, tenderhearted, forgiving one another, even as God for Christ's sake hath forgiven you."
Ephesians 4:32 KJV

"Not with eyeservice, as menpleasers; but as the servants of Christ, doing the will of God from the heart;"
Ephesians 6:6 KJV

"For this is thankworthy, if a man for conscience toward God endure grief, suffering wrongfully. For what glory is it, if, when ye be buffeted for your faults, ye shall take it patiently? But if, when ye do well, and suffer for it, ye take it patiently, this is acceptable with God."
I Peter 2:19 & 20 KJV

Personal Care

Regular cleaning and washing keeps germs at bay, and help keep our appearance beautiful. No matter what your age or what you look like, proper hygiene is one of the ways to keep our body as a healthy and attractive temple of the Lord.

Teeth – Keeping our teeth clean requires daily attention.

> Daily brushing
> Daily flossing
> Regular Dental checkups

Hair – It's important for a young lady to know how to care for her hair properly. Different people have different types of hair – yours may be long or short, curly, very curly, or straight. Your hair could be very thick, thin, fine or heavy. But sometimes our hair can be a source of discontentment. You may admire how your friend wears her hair, but find it impossible to do the same with your own hair – and all because your hair is different than hers. It seems that if we have long, thick hair we wish for short sleek hair, or if we have curly hair we wish for straight, or if we have fine hair we wish that it was heavier. One of the best things you can do to be content with your own hair is to learn to care for it so that it is attractive and enhancing to your God-given beauty.

> Keep your hair clean
> Keep your hair tidy
> Style your hair in a way that is becoming to you
> It is wise not to share your comb, brush or hat with others

Skin – Your skin can be one of the biggest problem areas in your personal hygiene. A girl's skin changes constantly – with age, from season to season, and from week to week during the month. Some days your skin may be very oily and prone to blemishes, and other days it may be dry and smooth all day. There are many products on the market for keeping your skin "blemish free", and you might try some of them to see if they work for you. But again, just like for your teeth and hair, there are some basic steps to take to keep your skin healthy.

> Keep your skin clean
> Keep your skin soft
> Keep your skin protected from the harsh sun
> Shower or bathe often

For lovely lips, speak words of kindness –
For a lovely face, that shines with grace,
walk with the knowledge that God is the Lord.
~ A Wise Old Proverb

From the quaint and treasured pages of a book from yesteryear, written to girls regarding "keeping house", we find methods that were taught to young girls and bits about how the home was kept long ago. Read on for snippets of wisdom from Grandmother Foster:

TOILET ARTICLES

"Of course my girls will take especial pride in the care of the washstand and dresser. Wash the toilet articles every morning after using, clean and dry the bowl, wipe out the soap dish, and carry out the slop-jar when you go after fresh water, if you have not a bath-room. Straighten up the top of the dresser, put pins, needles and hairpins in cushions, lay collars and ribbons in boxes, (for I am sure you all delight in keeping your drawers in beautiful order), set toilet bottles, manicure articles, brushes, etc., in place, and wipe away every particle of dust. Also use the dusting cloth on every other piece of furniture, and wipe off all the woodwork. Pull all the window shades down the same distance, and straighten up any books, pictures and magazines you may have about. Then step to the door, just as if you were a stranger, take a look about you and unless I am greatly mistaken you will be surprised to see how much improvement you have made in your room."

THE BATH-ROOM

"If your house has running water, you certainly must learn how to clean the bathroom! First of all, remove the rug, sweep up the dust, and wipe the floor with a damp cloth. Take the scouring soap and wash out the bath-tub, being sure to get off the ring that settles around the edge if the water is at all hard. When all nice and white, rinse out with fresh water and wipe dry. Next scour the top of the washstand and the faucets, wipe off any particles of soap, wash out the bowl and wipe it dry. If the toilet needs attention, make a stiff roll of an old newspaper and clean it with the end of that, flushing frequently so that you can see your are getting it clean. You do not need to even wet your hands by doing it this way, but when it is done wrap up the paper in dry piece, and take it downstairs to be burned or carried away. Polish the bath-room mirror and window, remove all soiled and wet linen, put out fresh towels, wipe the dust from the molding, and after shaking and sweeping the mat outside, spread it down in front of the bath tub."

Excerpted from Housekeeping, Cookery, Sewing for Little Girls by Olive H. Foster, circa 1922

Cozy & Inviting Kitchens

A Guide to Keeping
a Cozy & Inviting Kitchen
in the Home

My dear girls ~

There are five virtues that a homemaker must cultivate:

Order, Service, Honesty, Thrift and Industry.

Order means not only that there is a place for everything and everything is in its place, but also that there is a time for everything, and everything is done in its time.

Service means that our time, our tasks and our energy are used to serve others, and through serving others we serve Christ Himself.

Honesty means that we are honest with ourselves and others. We continually examine ourselves to see where we need to improve our skills, and we are also honest in our dealings with our families and neighbors.

Thrift does not mean cheap. Sometimes the thrifty way to do something isn't the cheapest way, but in the long run it is the way that saves us time and money.

Industry means that even when we would rather sit and rest, we do what needs to be done next and save the resting for when the work is done.

> *"Yet a little sleep, a little slumber, a little folding of the hands to sleep; so shall thy poverty come as one that travalleth, and thy want as an armed man."* Proverbs 6: 10-11

All five of these virtues are put to good use in your home. I hope you enjoy these lessons as you go through the days, weeks and months in the kitchen with your MotherDear!

- *Aunt Sophie*

Cozy & Inviting Kitchens
Home Skills Checklist

I can confidently do a good job and show responsibility in the kitchen by knowing the skills needed in the home regarding:

____ How to wash dishes
____ How to load & use an automatic electric dishwasher
____ How to deal with an emergency fire in the kitchen
____ How to write a menu
____ How to set a proper table
____ How to clean a kitchen floor
____ How to fix basic & simple meals
____ How to read & use recipes
____ Kitchen hygiene and cleanliness
____ Proper disposal of kitchen scraps & trash
____ Kitchen safety
____ How to use basic kitchen appliances
____ Begin my own recipe collection (notebook or card box)
____ Understand basic cooking terms
____ How to clean major kitchen appliances
____ Purchase my "first" cookbook for my collection
    CookBook Title:_____Purchase Date:_____
____ Begin to assist MotherDear in grocery shopping
____ Study a book on basic nutrition
    Enter Book Title:_____

NAME: _____
has passed the requirements for our home listed above and has proven herself a capable keeper of a home.

Signed:

MotherDear

Cozy & Inviting Kitchens
Home Skills Scheduling Chart

DAILY

Empty dishwasher (if applicable)
Preparations or planning for the daily main meal
Wash dishes
Wipe off kitchen countertops
Clean kitchen sink
Sweep kitchen floor
Empty garbage can
Replace dish cloth and towels with fresh ones

WEEKLY

Wipe down small appliances (toaster, microwave, etc.)
Remove items from counters and wipe thoroughly, include stovetop
Clean kitchen window & sill
Clean refrigerator: discard leftovers & wipe down inside, outside & top.
Sweep & mop the kitchen floor
Write out menus & shopping list for next week

MONTHLY

Clean stove range hood & filter
Dust corners and ceilings
Wipe down cupboard doors & shelves
Clean and organize some cupboards and drawers
Clean inside and outside of refrigerator & trash & compost cans.

SEASONALLY

Clean windows and wash curtains & blinds
Clean oven, refrigerator and other large appliances (inside, outside, under & over!)
Clean light fixtures
Organize and tidy pantry—heavy clean if necessary

Skills for Daily Cleaning

Aunt Sophie likes her daily tasks to have a rhythm and a pace that makes it feels like she's dancing through her day! A lot of time is spent in her kitchen every day - it is the hub of her home. She prepares meals for her family, bakes bread, cans and freezes garden produce for the winter, and plans future meals. Her key to keeping everything running smoothly is planning and order. Her routine will help you learn to manage your own kitchen and make it Cozy, clean, & inviting!

There are eight items on Aunt Sophie's daily checklist for the kitchen:

- **Empty dishwasher (if applicable)**

- **Preparations for the main meal of the day**

- **Wash dishes**

- **Wipe off the kitchen countertops**

- **Clean kitchen sink**

- **Sweep kitchen floor**

- **Empty garbage can**

- **Replace dish cloth and towels with fresh ones**

Empty dishwasher:
You may wonder why this task is the first on the list! Well, the last thing Aunt Sophie did in the kitchen the evening before was to start the dishwasher with the dirty dishes in it. Then the dishes are clean and ready to put away first thing in the morning. If your kitchen doesn't have a dishwasher, then skip this step.

Preparation & plans for the main meal of the day:
If you have kept up with Aunt Sophie's checklists, you wrote a menu for this week during your weekly chores last week, and you should have all of the ingredients for your meals available to use. Look at your menu for the day after tomorrow. Is there anything you need to remove from the freezer so it can thaw in the refrigerator? Look at your menu for tomorrow. Is there anything you need to prepare ahead of time? Do you have all the

ingredients you need on hand? Now look at your menu for today's main meal. If meat needed to be thawed, it should be in your refrigerator now. Check your recipe, and see how long it will take you to make this meal. Is it a crock pot meal? Then go ahead and start it now. Otherwise, make a note of what time today you need to start cooking or baking. If you make preparations early on in the day it will make the day run so much smoother.
The rest of Aunt Sophie's daily tasks are done after the evening meal.

Wash dishes:
Even though she has a dish washer, there are always some dishes that Aunt Sophie washes by hand in the sink. Since there are very few of them, this is usually a quick task. If your home is not equipped with this convenient appliance, the dishes can pile up quickly. So take time through the day to keep them washed up. Washing up dishes you use while you are cooking and baking, makes clean up time later, much faster. Keeping dirty dishes rinsed and organized, instead of piled and jumbled in the sink, is a good habit to form.

Wipe off kitchen countertops:
After the dishes are washed, Aunt Sophie sprays her counters with all-purpose disinfecting cleaner and wipes them clean. She uses the dish cloth to wipe them clean, rinsing as needed.

Clean kitchen sink:
Since Aunt Sophie cleans her sink every day, it doesn't take much scrubbing to keep it clean. Just spray the inside of the sink with your all-purpose cleaner, and rub it down. Then do the same with your faucets and the edge of your sink. Wipe it with your dish towel to dry it, and then put the towel and dish cloth in the laundry.

Sweep kitchen floor:
This task is another one that is done very quickly. Aunt Sophie keeps her broom and dustpan on a hook in a handy spot. It is quick and easy to sweep under the cabinets, in front of the stove and refrigerator, and gather all the dust and dirt into the center of the floor. Then sweep the dirt into the dust pan and empty the dust pan into the garbage can. While you're sweeping, be careful not to "flip" the broom and make the dust fly into the air!

Empty garbage can:
Aunt Sophie always makes sure she uses a plastic can liner to keep the inside of her garbage can clean. Empty the trash and replace the liner.

Replace dish cloth and towels:
The last thing Aunt Sophie does before leaving the kitchen for the night is to lay out a clean dish cloth, dish towel, and replace the hand towel. She starts the dishwasher, turns off the light, and her kitchen is ready for bed!

Washing Dishes 101

Every day in every household there are dishes to be washed! Dishwashing can be made a lot easier if you will take care to do it in an orderly fashion. Make it a habit to wash the dirtied dishes, pots, and pans after each meal and during the meal preparations. If this isn't possible, it is a must to at least rinse and stack them in a neat fashion or soak them in a large dishpan of warm water.

■ Using a tray or serving cart bring all the dirty dishes to the area near the kitchen sink. Lightly scrape all the soiled dishes into a scrap bin. Rinse any heavily soiled or greasy dishes with hot water. This helps keep your dishwater reasonably clean until all the dishes are finished.

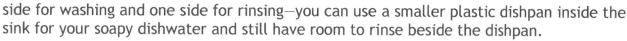

■ Put a stopper in the drain and fill your sink half-full of hot water—adding in a small squeeze of liquid dish soap while the water is running to make some sudsy bubbles. If you do not have a double kitchen sink—one side for washing and one side for rinsing—you can use a smaller plastic dishpan inside the sink for your soapy dishwater and still have room to rinse beside the dishpan.

■ The efficient order for washing is glasses and cups first, silverware next; then plates, serving dishes and lastly the pots and pans and other cooking utensils

■ Take care to wash, scrubbing if necessary, to get dishes spit-spot and rinsing each one well in hot water .

■ Hot water and a good soap is what is needed to cut the grease and grime on dirty dishes. Using a pair of rubber gloves if you wash lots of dishes saves your hands and keeps them protected from the hot water.

■ If pots or pans have stubborn stuck-on foods, fill with an inch of water in the bottom and add in 2 tablespoons of baking soda and return to the stove and boil the water over medium heat until it is loosened.

■ If there is excess grease in a pan always dump it first and wipe down the surface to remove as much as you can with a paper towel before washing it up.

■ Cast iron skillets usually need only scrubbing with hot water and then dry thoroughly and lightly oil the surface wiping the oil around with a paper towel before storing it for the next use.

■ Never drop sharp knives into the dishwater, but wash them carefully, one at a time, keeping the sharp edge away from your hand.

■ When washing up electric skillets and other appliances — NEVER immerse in water! Read your instructions that came with the appliance before any washing or cleaning.

■ Place all washed, rinsed dishes into a dish drainer or laid out carefully on a clean towel. Glasses and cups can all be placed upside down and plates lined up carefully in the drainer.

■ Dishes can be dried with a clean, soft, absorbent towel or air-dried. Always put away each dish back into its own "home" when they are completely dry.

The Kitchen Sink:

Aunt Sophie likes to keep her kitchen sink sparkling clean. Choose a time once a week to be nice to your sink and get it shiny clean. Day after day it is in constant use and needs extra care and effort to keep it spit-spot! Empty the sink and put away the dish drainer. [Aunt Sophie keeps hers in the cupboard under the sink.] Sprinkle the inside of the sink with baking soda, and scrub with your dish cloth. Be sure to clean the back splash behind the faucets, around the faucets, and the counter around the sink. Rinse the sink well. Now take your window cleaner and spray your sink and faucet. Wipe the whole area dry with your dish towel. Now your dish cloth and towel are ready to go into the laundry. They've been working hard!

The Dishwasher's Delight:

Most kitchens of today are equipped with modern automatic dishwashers. These help save time and work; keep the kitchen free of stacks of dishes, as dirty dishes can be stored inside until ready for a wash cycle, and they use extremely hot water that sanitizes the dishes. No hand drying is needed as an automatic dishwasher has high temperatures that dries the dishes after washing and rinsing. What a boon to the one who is designated the job of dish washer!

To use an automatic dishwasher: Always read the instructions that came with the particular dishwasher you use or become familiar with it with instructions from MotherDear and follow these steps for auto dishwashing:

■ Lightly scrape off any excess food.
■ Rinse under warm water dishes that have any heavy residues on them.
■ Load the dishwasher, putting the dishes in the correct areas according the manual.
■ Add the dishwashing detergent in the correct receptacle—this is not the same as dish soap!
■ Close the door securely and latch it if it has a lock-latch and then turn it on. Most dish washers have a choice of cycles as in "normal" "pot scrubber" or to turn off the drying setting. Use "normal" unless you know to set it differently.
■ When it has completed its cycles—your dishes are sparkling clean and dry and ready for to be stored in their proper places.

What is compost?

If you grow a backyard garden with vegetables and herbs, save all the kitchen scraps like potato peelings, egg shells, over-ripe fruits, pretty much anything but grease and meat products. Put all these scraps into a covered container and once every few days empty it into a designated area out of doors near the garden area. Add yard leaves and grass clippings into this pile and as you allow it to sit and decompose it miraculously turns into nice rich black dirt that is very good to add to your herbs and vegetable plots. Stirring it up with a big garden fork every so often quickens the time it takes for it to break down into rich dark crumbly dirt that is good food for your garden plants but even if left alone—it will eventually compost itself. Homemade compost is a wonderful way to recycle the kitchen scraps!

Kitchen Tips:

It is best to use old raggedy dish towels for cleaning days and not fresh new ones!

Use stale bread to make bread crumbs, using a food processor. Store in a baggie in the freezer and they can be used to add to meatloaf and for casserole crumb toppings.

" Even a child, I believe, feels the pleasure of going into a fresh, clean kitchen, and I want all my little housekeepers to learn how to keep things nice."
from Housekeeping, Cookery, Sewing for Little Girls by Olive Hyde Foster circa 1922

Skills for Weekly Cleaning

Aunt Sophie does her weekly checklist for the kitchen all in one day. Part of the orderliness that she likes to have in her home is "a time for everything, and everything done in its time," so Aunt Sophie always does her weekly kitchen cleaning on Wednesday morning. Wednesday may not be the best day of the week in your home to do these tasks, but choose one day and always do your kitchen cleaning on that day. If the day goes awry, tomorrow is another day! Here is Aunt Sophie's weekly checklist for the kitchen:

- **Wipe down small appliances (Toaster...etc.)**

- **Remove items from counters and wipe thoroughly, include stovetop**

- **Clean kitchen window & sill**

- **Clean refrigerator: discard leftovers & wipe down inside, outside, & top**

- **Sweep & mop kitchen floor**

- **Write out menus & shopping list**

Wipe down small appliances:

Appliances that are used on a regular basis need to be cleaned often. Attention to them once a week keeps them nice as new! Your home's kitchen may be equipped with some or all of these small appliances that are helpful tools in the home's kitchen. First, fill your sink with warm soapy water; have a wiping cloth and a drying cloth ready for use. Using older cloths and towels is best for clean up jobs instead of using pretty, newer kitchen cloths. Aunt Sophie cautions: "Always unplug appliances before cleaning!"

• **Microwave:** If there is a glass plate in the bottom of your microwave, remove it and wash it in the sink of soapy water. Then take your cloth, dip it in your sink of soapy water, wring it, and wipe the inside and outside of your microwave. Don't forget to do the top of the inside of the oven! Dry the plate and replace it.

• **Toaster:** Remove the crumb tray from the bottom of your toaster and wash it. To clean the outside of the toaster Aunt Sophie likes to use a paper towel and window cleaner. The window cleaner removes all of the burned on dirt and leaves the toaster shiny and clean. Dry the crumb tray and replace it.

• **Coffee Maker:** Remove the coffee pot, the filter basket (throw out any leftover grounds and filter that may be left from the morning), and any other easily removable parts and wash them. Rinse your cloth in the sink water, and use it to wipe the outside of the coffee maker, the burner, and the top where the filter usually is. Dry the parts that you washed and replace them.

For stubborn stains that accumulate over time, pour 2 cups of vinegar into the coffee maker and let it run through the brew cycle. Then follow it with 3 full cycles of water to flush out the vinegar. If extra scrubbing is needed, use a scrubbie pad and get off those coffee stains!

• **Large Kitchen Mixer:** Using your damp cloth, wipe the outside of your mixer.

• **Electric Grain Mill:** Remove the canister that holds the milled flour, if it is washable, hand wash and dry thoroughly. Wipe the outside of the mill with your damp cloth.

• **Blender, Food Processor, Electric Can Opener, etc.:** Any of these small appliances need to be wiped down on the outside. Remove parts and clean as necessary.

• **Dishwasher:** Even though this isn't one of her small appliances, Aunt Sophie cleans her dish washer at the same time as them. Use your damp cloth, wipe the edges of the door and make sure the food strainer at the bottom of the dishwasher is clear. Wipe the front of the dishwasher door, and then dry it with the dish towel.

Remove items from counters and wipe down:

Even though Aunt Sophie cleans her countertops every day, once a week she removes everything that is on the counters and washes the entire counter. Work on one area of your counter at a time. Remove everything that you store on that counter, and then wash with your dish cloth. Dry with your dish towel, and then replace the items. Work around your kitchen this way until all of the countertops have been thoroughly washed and dried. If your countertop has a backsplash, be sure to wipe the top of this, also.

Clean stove top: How you clean your stovetop depends on the type of stove.

• **Gas stove:** Remove grates and drip pans. Wash the drip pans in the sink, and use your cleaning cloth to wipe the rest of the stove surface. Dry the drip pans and replace them and the grates.

• **Electric stove [with coils]:** Tilt the coils up so you can remove the metal rings and drip pans. Some stoves require you to remove the coils (just pull gently) to remove the drip pans. Wash the rings and drip pans, using a pot scrubber and scouring powder to remove any stubborn spots, and use your cleaning cloth, rinsing your cloth as needed, to wipe and clean the rest of the stove surface.

• **Smooth top or glass top electric stove:** Use the cleaner recommended by the manufacturer Be sure to dry the top with your towel after cleaning it. While you're cleaning the stove top, also use your dish cloth the wipe the control panel and the front of the oven door. Dry with your dish towel.

Clean windows:

Aunt Sophie loves the window over her kitchen sink, but it is always getting splashed and is left with water spots on it. If you have a window in your kitchen, spray it with glass cleaner and wipe it with an old, crumpled newspaper or a paper towel. Don't forget to wipe down the sill.

Clean refrigerator:

Every family has leftover food. Aunt Sophie tries to use the leftovers in other dishes, or heats them up to eat for lunch, but usually there is leftover food that just doesn't get used. Take time once a week to go through the refrigerator and discard any old food. If you are prudent, there won't be very much to throw away during these weekly cleanings, but discard foods that are over a week old. [Of course, not the ketchup, pickles, mayonnaise, salad dressings, butter and jellies! But do check as most of these have expiration dates on them.] Many times, leftover scraps can be feed to farm animals. Aunt Sophie's laying hens love to peck at leftovers like rice! Be sure to check the fresh fruits and vegetables that are stored in the refrigerator, and discard any that are beginning to spoil. These can go straight to the compost so they are not a total waste!

Straighten the items in your refrigerator and make a note of any staples that need to be replenished when you do your weekly shopping. If needed wipe up any spills or spots inside with a damp soapy cloth.

Now Aunt Sophie takes her spray bottle of all-purpose cleaner and a damp cloth and cleans the outside of the refrigerator. Just spray the outside surface and rub clean with the cloth. Pay special attention to the handle of the door and the top of the refrigerator – both of these areas can be especially dirty.

Sweep & mop kitchen floor:

If you remember Aunt Sophie's daily checklist, you know that she sweeps her kitchen floor every evening. But once a week she uses her vacuum cleaner to get the dirt that her broom has missed. Using the hose attachment on your vacuum cleaner, vacuum under the cabinets, between the refrigerator and cabinets, under the front of the refrigerator and stove, and all the other crooks and crannies. Sweep the center of your floor. If the vacuum cleaner has a "bare floor" setting, use that. If not, use the broom and dust pan. Now that your floor has been swept, it's time to mop it. Aunt Sophie uses a bucket of water and floor cleaner for her kitchen floor. As you mop, start in the corner farthest from the door and work toward the door. Dirt accumulates around the sink, dishwasher and stove, so pay special attention to these spots. Small brushes and scrubbies with handles work well in these areas where dirt loves to sneak into and try to hide! Rinse your mop often, and wring the mop out so that it is damp rather than wet when you use it.

Write out menus and shopping list:

While the kitchen floor is drying, Aunt Sophie takes time to sit down and make the menu and grocery list for the next week.

First, Aunt Sophie decides what the main course will be for each day of the week. She tries to choose dishes that she knows her family likes, but will also be economical. Meals that include meat can be expensive, but they're also an important source of protein.

Vegetables, fruits and whole grains are also important for a balanced diet, and Aunt Sophie tries to include all of these things in her meals. So she varies the types of meals she provides for her family through the week to include different types of meats and dried beans used in casseroles, soups and sandwiches. (Dried beans when served with a grain like rice also make a complete protein!)

Aunt Sophie already has her menus for breakfasts and lunches planned (she planned these menus one time, and uses them every week). She looks through these menus to see if there is anything that will need to be changed or added for the coming week. Changes are nice for variety and are sometimes necessary when skimping for the food budget!

Next, Aunt Sophie decides what side dishes will go with each main dish. If the main dish is spaghetti with meat sauce, there is already protein, grain and one vegetable in the meal. She just needs to choose one more vegetable and a fruit to make this meal a balanced meal for her family. She goes through each day's menu in the same way, varying the vegetables and fruits so that she doesn't serve the same thing two days in a row.

Now she is ready to make her grocery list. Through the week as Aunt Sophie has used items from her pantry, she has written those items down on the grocery list she keeps on the refrigerator. Now she goes through the recipes she plans to use on her daily menus and adds the ingredient items needed for those meals. She also adds in any items that she might need for the breakfast and lunch menus.

Since Aunt Sophie does her shopping on Fridays, she puts her grocery list on refrigerator until shopping day. For the next two days she has an opportunity to add anything she may have forgotten, and when it's time to go to the store she just takes her grocery list off the refrigerator and she's ready to go.

MotherDear may choose to shop once a month and buy lots of basic food staples. If the family is large, it is a good time saver and more economical to shop this way. But, trips to the store each week are inevitable for items like milk and fresh fruits and vegetables. Aunt Sophie's kitchen is freshly cleaned, she has planned ahead and now she is ready for a new week!

Menu Planning

It is a worthwhile project to begin writing down favorite food combinations and practice planning menus. You can browse thru MotherDear's cookbook collection and even add some new dishes that sound tasty to your own menu plans. Begin with trying to write down a few simple menus for every day meals and some special menus for company fare. Having some traditional family holiday menus recorded is always nice too! Menus are merely a listing of the names of dishes or foods that will be served in one complete meal. A fancy holiday menu may look like this:

Baked Turkey

Granny's Stuffing

Sweet Potato Pone

Creamed Corn

Green Beans

Cranberry Freeze

Butterhorn Dinner Rolls & Honey

Carrot Cake with Cream Cheese Icing

Iced Tea & Coffee

A proper written menu begins with the main dish, next lists the side dishes, then list the complements like rolls or muffins, dessert, and lastly the beverages. If dishes are served together like "Tea & Coffee" they are listed on the same line. Otherwise each food is placed on a separate line. Always capitalize each named item on your menu. On any given menu you create, try to have variety in texture, color and flavor. Always consider your family's favorites, the foods available, the budget, and the season of the year. Hot soup is not always welcome on a hot summer day but is comforting and delicious on cold wintry days!

Mealtime Manners

♥ Always drink water by sipping it and not gulping!

♥ Do not pile your plate with food–take conservative portions considering those who have yet to be served.

♥ Always remember to use the gracious words of "Please" , "Thank you" and "Excuse me".

♥ Never reach across the table or in front of another seated for something. Ask for it be passed.

♥ Do not place bones and such (egg shells from boiled eggs) on the tablecloth or off your plate. Use a small extra "bone" plate for these scraps if necessary, otherwise leave on the edge of your plate.

♥ Try it—You might like it! If you wish to decline seconds or a food always say, "No, thank you".

Wisdom from Grandmother Foster:

"Every mother should begin to instruct her little daughter at an early age in the different branches of housekeeping, and if taught in the right way, none will prove more attractive than cooking. When quite young the child will be eager to experiment, and generally will be careful; and with many of the simple recipes she can scarcely make a mistake, and they will prove invaluable to her later on. Cooking is of great educational value. Aside from giving a girl that knowledge necessary to the proper conduct of a home, in the dexterous handling of utensils and food products, the concentration required, and the practice of doing certain work for certain results, it also gives excellent mental training and brings all-around development. Every girl should strive to become a good practical cook; and in the majority of cases, for many reasons, MotherDear is the best teacher."

Cookery for Little Girls circa 1922

Menus & Marketing

To plan a menu (which is a written listing of what is served and prepared for a meal) it is best to decide first on the main dish and then add foods around that main dish which will complement it. In many families menus are passed down over the years. In Grandmother's kitchen, if she serves salmon patties, she always has ketchup on the table for dipping, macaroni & cheese as a side dish, green beans as a vegetable and cold, sweet applesauce. The meal should be tasty and flavorful and look pretty on the plate. Remember these main considerations when menu planning:

Do not repeat flavors and colors on the same menu. If you are having carrots that are orange, do not serve sweet potatoes too! If you are having apple and raisin salad, no apple pie for dessert, please!

Combine different shapes of food on your menu. Long green beans, kernels of corn, meat balls, mashed potatoes, garlic toast - all are varieties that could be served in one meal.

At least one hot food is best served at each main meal. Serve hot food, hot and cold food, well chilled. There are some exceptions like leftover ham or turkey that are good cold or hot.

Don't serve all soft foods or all crispy harder foods. Variety is the key! Crispy crackers with soups, mashed potatoes with fried chicken. Babies, of course, get all mashed foods that are soft until they get their little teeth in place!

Look over the menus for the week ahead and check the pantry and cupboards, refrigerator and freezer. Make the marketing list for all ingredients needed to prepare the meals. Making a neat and organized market list is very helpful in making the marketing to go smoothly. If you are shopping at a grocery market where you have shopped often you will become familiar with where items are located. Group your list on paper helps to organize the shopping. Make your list with the headings:

MEATS

FROZEN

FRESH PRODUCE

DAIRY CASE

CANNED GOODS

BASIC DRY GOODS

SPICES ...and so on.

Going to the market takes a lot of time and after everything is purchased it still has to be brought home and put away neatly in the cupboards, refrigerator, or freezer. Plan a special day for marketing and try to make menus around items that are on sale and are a good bargain. Learn to make some basic simple meals you and your family will like and practice on those, ro- tating them so they don't tire of them. As you become a more efficient and accomplished cook you can begin to try new recipes!

Every girl needs her own recipe collection. Begin by either typing or writing out simple favorite recipes from MotherDear, Aunties, or Grandmothers. Fill a 3 ring binder with your recipe pages. If you would like, you can decorate a small box and write and record favorite recipes on small lined cards instead of using a binder. Whether using a binder or card box be sure to make divided categories so you can easily find your favorite recipe as your collection grows!

The Family Table

When the table is set neatly and attractively it creates a nice atmosphere. This is something that can be done for the family meal by little kitchen helpers (brothers & sisters) or something you can do for MotherDear if she is fixing the meal. There are some necessary items needed to set a table like a fork and a plate but noth- ing needs to be elaborate. You can make it cheery and inviting with a little imagination. Here are some ideas to make a nice table for your family.

Use a tablecloth table runner or placemats. A tablecloth can be as simple as a pretty, flat bed sheet. If you want to keep it for a tablecloth, you can lay it on the table, then draw around the outline of the table with chalk. Lay it on the floor and measure down 6"-9" from the chalk line. Make a new chalk mark all the way around at the 9" mark from your first chalk line. Cut on the second chalk line. Get some pretty lace or trim from your sewing goods store and stitch around the bottom of your table cloth.

If you do not have a big piece of fabric you can cut a square 36" x 36" and trim the edges or just hem it. You can lay this in the center or any table with the corners pointing to each end of the table. Set a basket of fruit in the middle and you have a pretty table!

Pretty tea towels can be bought and used for place mats. They are placed at each place and symmetrically spaced. Napkins can be paper or cloth. At one time we purchased soft matching washcloths. We used them daily for mealtime napkins. An old-fashioned stick clothespin was painted with a permanent marker with a tiny face on the head of the clothes- pin. Then each family member's name was lettered down the length of the pin. We pinned each washcloth with a personalized clothespin and kept them in a basket near the table. After the meal they were dampened to wipe up dirty little hands and faces, if this was needed, and then they were thrown into the washer. When washed and dried they were re-pinned and put back in the basket to be used for the next mealtime. Whatever you use on your tabletop, be sure it is CLEAN and WRINKLE-FREE.

A centerpiece is a nice addition to the table. It can be as simple as a small, green plant in a pretty pot. You could try a small grouping of candles or an oil lamp. Be sure to keep your centerpiece low enough and in proportion to the table size so you can see and talk to each other unobstructed. Even a simple canning jar with a bow around the neck, filled with fresh picked flowers from the woods, is very pretty. Use your imagination and make your table SPECIAL!

Excerpted with permission from "Marmee's Kitchen Primer" A first textbook on cooking and keeping a proper kitchen

Advanced Dinner Assignment

Let's have Company!

MENU:
Parmesan Chicken
Corn on the Cob
Seven Layer Salad
Angel Biscuits w/ Honey Butter
Lemonade with Tea Cubes Brownies

On separate sheets of paper make a shopping list of all the ingredients you will need to serve this dinner using the recipes provided here. Keep your receipts and attach them to the shopping list after returning home. Divide the cost of the ingredients by the number of people served at this meal and put down how much this meal cost to serve per person:
COST PER PERSON: $ _____

On another sheet of paper list all the kitchen equipment and utensils you will need to prepare & serve this dinner. Even include "oven" for baking the chicken and refrigerator for keeping the salad chilled etc. Don't forget to include the tableware for eating.

Arrange in sequence the list below as to how they need to be accomplished to serve this dinner on schedule. Then recopy it in correct numbered sequence on a separate sheet.

Time to serve the meal: _____ O'clock   Day & Date:_____

Prepare lemonade ___
Coat chicken pieces ___
Make biscuit dough ___
Wash, chop and slice all salad fixings ___
Fry bacon, crumble ___
Prepare the table ___
Invite the company to dinner ___
Cut lemon slices ___
Wash up dinner dishes ___
Bake parmesan chicken ___
Put together 7 layer salad & garnish ___
Cover and set salad in refrigerator to chill ___
Cook corn on the cob ___

Serve the food buffet style ___
Freeze tea cubes ___
Mix together layer salad dressing ___
Make honey-butter spread ___
Bake brownies ___
Shop at the grocery for the company meal ___
Bring a pot of water to boil for corn cobs ___
Thaw chicken pieces (if frozen) ___
Place prepared food into serving dishes ___
Pour lemonade into glasses and garnish ___
Shuck and silk fresh corn on cob (if applies) ___
Bake biscuits ___
Prepare tea w/ spices ___

Think ahead! Your brownies can be made a day in advance to make things simpler on the day you will serve company. Bacon can be fried and crumbled early in the day and refrigerated. Beverage can certainly made ahead and stay refrigerated and cubes frozen early on. It is best to market ahead of time and not on the same day of the preparations. Take care to arrange the table. Set a pretty cloth on it— if you don't have one, a flat, brightly colored, clean, and freshly pressed bed sheet works in a pinch! Some pretty placemats make a cheerful and neat table setting too. Be creative and make a centerpiece for the table. If you don't have an idea for one - how about a pretty bowl of fresh plump lemons and limes edged with some large green leaves? Plan ahead; be creative; follow your tried and true recipes carefully; keep things orderly and clean; your dinner will be a great success!

Company Dinner Recipes

Parmesan Chicken

Mix in a bowl:
2 cups of instant potato flakes
2 tablespoons parsley flakes
4 tablespoons Parmesan cheese
pinch of salt and black pepper
Melt 1 stick butter in a small saucepan. Dip 16 skinless chicken pieces in melted butter. Melt more butter if needed. Sprinkle butter-coated chicken pieces with salt. Then coat each chicken piece in potato-flake mixture. Place chicken pieces, close together, on foil-lined baking sheets in one single layer. Bake for 1 hour and 15 minutes at 400° or until crispy and lightly browned. Turn chicken pieces once after 40 minutes so both sides brown evenly. [Serves 12-14]

Seven Layer Salad

Layer in a large, oblong glass dish in the order listed:
1 head iceberg or romaine lettuce, shredded
2 stalks celery, diced
1 cup sweet green bell pepper, diced
1 medium red sweet onion, thinly sliced
2 cups English peas (Run warm water over frozen English peas to thaw slightly, pat dry; or use fresh raw garden peas).
Mix together in a small bowl:
1 1/2 cups mayonnaise + 2 teaspoons sugar
Spread over layers carefully. Sprinkle grated Cheddar cheese generously over dressing layer. Top salad with crumbled, crisply-cooked bacon. Garnish all sides with small cherry tomatoes. Cover with plastic wrap and refrigerate until serving. [Serves 10-12]

Angel Biscuits

Place in a small bowl, stir and set aside:
1 heaping tablespoon yeast + 5 tablespoons warm water (110°)
Place in a large mixing bowl:
5 cups unbleached all-purpose flour + 1/4 cup sugar 4 teaspoons baking powder + 1 teaspoon salt
Mix dry ingredients until blended and then cut in shortening until you have coarse crumbs:
1 cup vegetable shortening
Add in to crumbly flour mixture:
1 1/2 cups warm buttermilk (110°) + yeast mixture that was set aside
Stir to combine and turn out onto a floured surface. Knead by hand, lightly, about 6 times. Pat out to a 1/2-inch thickness. Cut out with a biscuit cutter and transfer to a large, greased baking sheet. Let biscuits stand on baking sheets for 15 minutes and then bake for 20 minutes at 400° or until golden brown on tops. Downsize recipe in half for a smaller batch. [Yield approx. 30 biscuits]

Brownie Bars

Place into a large mixing bowl and stir to combine:
2 cups sugar
4 eggs, beaten
3/4 cup cooking oil
1/2 cup unsweetened baking cocoa powder
1 3/4 cups unbleached all-purpose flour
1 teaspoon salt
1 teaspoon vanilla extract

Place batter into a well-greased 9"x 13" baking pan. Sprinkle top of batter with 1 1/2 cups chocolate chips. Bake for 25-35 minutes at 350°. Do not over bake. Check for doneness around edges. Let cool and cut into bars. [Makes 15-18 bars]

Corn-on-the-Cob

Have a large pot of water boiling on the stove. Drop in corn cobs that have been shucked and washed free of silks. You may also put frozen ears of corn in the boiling water. There is no need to thaw them. Let simmer 7-10 minutes and serve hot with butter and salt. Allow 1 ear per person.

Lemonade with Tea Cubes

Heat together in a small saucepan, stirring until sugar dissolves: 1 cup sugar + 4 cups water
Cool and then stir in: Juice of 8 lemons

To serve: Fill tall glasses with tea cubes. Pour lemonade over cubes and garnish each glass with lemon slices. Multiply recipe as needed to make larger quantities
Pour into a pitcher. Refrigerate. Place in small saucepan and bring to boil: 3 cups water + 15 whole cloves + 4 (2-inch) cinnamon sticks Remove from heat and pour over 8 regular-size tea bags. Let stand for 10 minutes. Discard spices and tea bags and add in: 3 cups cold water. Pour into ice cube trays and freeze. [Makes approximately 4 trays of tea cubes]

How to Use a Recipe

Always read a recipe through from the start to the finish before you begin to use it.

Always find all the ingredients in the recipe and set them on a tray or the counter close to where you will prepare it. As you use an ingredient in the recipe set it aside. This aids in not forgetting an ingredient or making a mistake by adding it twice!

Always use standard measuring spoons and cups and learn the abbreviations found in many recipes for these standard measures

Tbsp. = stands for tablespoon measure
tsp. = stands for a teaspoon measure

These are not be confused. One tablespoon is equal to three teaspoons. Always use the standard measuring spoons when making a recipe. Usually the table- spoon will be abbreviated with a capital "T" and have the "b" in it so you can differentiate between it and a standard teaspoon. Do not confuse these with tableware that is used for eating. A set of measuring spoons is an essential for a cook and baker at home. At times you will see a "c." which is abbreviated for cup, meaning a standard cup measure. Standard cup measures come in 1/4; 1/3; 1/2; and a whole cup. Do not confuse a liquid measuring cup with a spout with dry measuring cups. Use measuring cups with marked increments and a spout for measuring liquids only. Measurements in recipes must be level and exact or you risk a "flop".

DOUBLE or Downsize?

At times you will find a recipe and want to cook it for a larger group or possibly only make a small amount of what it yields. To halve a recipe divide every single ingredient measure by 2. To increase a recipe multiply every ingredient by 2 or 3. Be cautious in working with doubling or downsizing as some particular recipes don't work well with larger or smaller amounts than specified. If you are cutting a recipe in half and it calls for only one egg, beat the egg and then measure it into equal portions using a spoon into 2 separate cups. Use only one of them and try to find a use for the other portion of beaten egg.

PROJECT ASSIGNMENT:

Find 2 simple recipes and double one and downsize the other one by half. Be sure to record your new measurements beside the original ones in a different color ink or using [ ] around the new measurement. (Try this on your own first, but if you need help getting started, see the example answers on the last page in this section.)

Skills for Monthly Cleaning

Once a month, Aunt Sophie spends extra time in the kitchen. The monthly chores are a bit harder and more time consuming than the weekly chores, so Aunt Sophie sets aside a separate day for them. Even though these chores are bigger, the same principle applies - by keeping up with the daily and weekly chores, even the biggest jobs are quick and easy. Here is Aunt Sophie's monthly checklist for her kitchen:

- Clean & organize kitchen cupboards & drawers (a few each month)
- Sweep ceiling and corners
- Clean stove range hood & filter
- Clean refrigerator
- Clean dishwasher
- Clean kitchen garbage can and compost container

Clean and organize the inside of your cupboards:
This is one of those big chores that needs to be broken down into smaller pieces. Count the number of cupboards in your kitchen, both top and bottom. Divide that number by six and you have the number of cupboards that you should clean each month. That way all of your cupboards are cleaned and organized twice a year.

To clean your cupboards, start by emptying one of them completely. Wipe out the inside of the shelves and the side and back walls. You can replace the shelf liner if it needs it, but it probably won't need it every time.

Now start replacing the items in the cupboard. If there is something you don't use or don't want to keep, find another home for it. Organize the cupboard so that it is easy to reach the things you use often. Remember to empty and clean only one cupboard at a time or you will make more of a mess and be overwhelmed!

Clean and organize drawers:
This is another chore where you will divide the number of your drawers by six, and clean only one or two each month. Do this chore the same way you cleaned the cupboards.

Clean the outside of the cupboards and drawers:
Use your all-purpose cleaner, or if your cabinet fronts are wood, you can use a special wood cleaner. Pay special attention to the cabinets near the dishwasher, sink and stove, as these are more likely to be splashed during cooking and clean up. If you have a large kitchen, you may want to divide this chore up the way you did for cleaning the inside of the cupboards and drawers, but be sure to clean the extra dirty ones each month.

Sweep ceiling and wall corners:
This is one of those fun chores, and if you remember, we do this same chore as part of our

monthly cleaning in the bathroom. Take a soft cloth and wrap it around the bristle end of your broom. Aunt Sophie uses an old towel and fastens it with a safety pin to hold in on. Now gently sweep along the corners of the room where the walls and ceilings meet. This catches any cobwebs before they have a chance to show!

Clean range hood and filter:

The hood above your stove can be a very dirty place if you don't clean it regularly. The dust that accumulates there tends to be greasy, so it needs more than just a dust cloth to clean it. Aunt Sophie dusts the inside of the hood with a damp paper towel sprayed with her all-purpose cleaner. Then she removes the filter and cleans it with warm, soapy water in the sink. Sometimes a special de-greaser cleaner is needed in the water. Rinse the filter and let it air dry before replacing it.

Clean the refrigerator:

Once a month Aunt Sophie cleans the inside of her refrigerator thoroughly. Start by turning your refrigerator off. Then move the food out of the refrigerator into a cooler. If you don't have a cooler, then put the food on a counter - but work very quickly so that you can put the food back into the refrigerator as soon as possible. If you have wire shelves in your refrigerator, remove then. If you have glass shelves, remove them and wash them in the sink just as you would wash dishes, and wash the produce bins and any other items that can be removed. Then wash the walls, top, bottom and inside door of the refrigerator with your dish cloth, or use your all-purpose cleaner. Replace the shelves and the food and turn your refrigerator back on. Be sure to check it in about ten minutes to make sure it's returning to the correct temperature. Repeat the process with the freezer section of your refrigerator.

Clean the dishwasher:

It seems like you wouldn't need to clean your dishwasher since its job is to clean things, but Aunt Sophie knows that every dishwasher can develop a build up of mineral deposits and soap residue that keeps it from working as well as it should. During your monthly cleaning, pour a cup of white vinegar into the bottom of your empty dishwasher and run it on a normal cycle. If your dishwasher has an option that heats the water, use that also. You'll be surprised at how fresh and clean your dishwasher is when it's done!

Clean the kitchen garbage can:

This is the last chore on Aunt Sophie's monthly list. If you always use a liner in your kitchen garbage can, then this chore won't be too hard. First, empty the garbage can. If the weather is pleasant, you can just squirt a little dishwashing soap into the bottom of the can, then take it outside and use the hose to wash it out. Otherwise, using your all-purpose cleaner and a paper towel wipe out the inside of the can. When it is dry, replace the liner. Aunt Sophie's kitchen garbage can has a lid that also needs to be cleaned. Even though Aunt Sophie keeps the outside of the lid cleaned daily, the inside – where we never see – can accumulate a lot of dirt. You can wash the lid in the sink just as you did the refrigerator shelves. If you are keeping a container in your kitchen to collect compost scraps—it needs a good washing every month. Empty it completely into the compost pile outdoors and then wash it thoroughly with hot soapy water. Dry it with a towel and put it back in its place.

Skills for Seasonal Cleaning

There are two jobs that Aunt Sophie does at the beginning of each new season. She adds them to her monthly chores, or sometimes waits until a separate cleaning time to do them.

- **Clean oven**

- **Clean window curtains and blinds**

Clean the oven:

This is one of those jobs that needs to be done regularly. An oven is much easier to clean if it isn't too dirty, but it is a real chore if you put it off. Aunt Sophie knows that a clean oven is also much more pleasant to use.

There are times when your oven will need to be cleaned even though it isn't the scheduled time to do it. If you have recently roasted a turkey, for example, there will probably be grease spattered on the inside of the oven. Or sometimes a pie or casserole will run over and spill on the oven floor. In these situations, it is best to clean the oven as soon as possible or else the spilled food will burn the next time you turn the oven on. Otherwise, cleaning the oven once every three months should be sufficient.

Before cleaning your oven remove the racks and wash them in warm, soapy water. Lay them aside until your oven is clean.

There are various types of ovens, and you should be sure to be aware of the type of oven in your home. If you have a self-cleaning oven, read the instructions very carefully before using the clean cycle. The way a self-cleaning oven works is that it gets extremely hot and burns the food residue on the inside of the oven. Because of this, the oven needs to be locked while it is in its cleaning cycle. A self-cleaning oven is also very well insulated because of the great amount of heat that is generated.

Before starting the self-cleaning cycle, wipe up any spilled food that might be on the bottom of the oven. Run the cleaning cycle according to your oven's instructions. It will last 3 to 6 hours. Starting the cleaning cycle in the evening after supper is usually a good time, because you can check on it during the cleaning to make sure everything is going well, and then it can cool overnight. After the oven is cool, unlock it (some ovens lock and unlock automatically) and wipe out the inside with a damp paper towel. You will be wiping up the ashes left from the cleaning. Replace the racks, and your oven is ready to use again.

If you have a standard oven without the self-clean feature, you will need to use an oven cleaner. One option is to use a commercial oven cleaning product. Be sure to read the instructions on the can and make sure you kitchen is well ventilated.

Another option is to make your own cleaner. Mix 1/4 cup water, 1/4 cup salt and 3/4 cup baking soda in a bowl to make a paste. Wipe down the inside of the oven with a wet cloth to get it damp, then spread the paste on the walls, top and bottom. Let it sit overnight and wipe it out in the morning. It can be messy, but much safer than commercial products.

More Tips from Grandmother Foster:

"In the kitchen you will probably notice that a layer of greasy dust collects very quickly on everything. This is because in cooking part of the solid matter is carried off with the steam and settles everywhere, catching and holding the dust. This is hard to get off, and will probably require scrubbing with warm water, good soap, and a little borax or ammonia to cut the grease. Wash only a small surface at a time, so that the alkali in the soap will not injure any painted or varnish surfaces, rinse with clear water, and wipe perfectly dry. If you don't wipe dry, the water catches the dust."

from Housekeeping, Cookery, Sewing for Little Girls by Olive Hyde Foster circa 1922

Clean the window curtains or blinds:

Aunt Sophie likes to have a lace curtain to dress up her kitchen window. Your home may have cloth curtains or perhaps you have blinds at the window. Aunt Sophie makes sure that she washes her curtains every three months to keep them fresh and clean.

If your window has curtains, just take them off the curtain rod and run them through the washing machine. It is best to always use washable fabrics when sewing up the kitchen curtains as they will certainly need to be washed many times over!

If you have blinds you can wash them in the bathtub. Fill the bathtub with 2 to 3 inches of warm, soapy water. Dish washing soap works well. Remove the blinds from their holders on the window, and put them into the water. Make sure the water covers them completely and let them soak for about a half hour. Gently swish the blinds back and forth in the water to remove all of the dust and dirt. Empty the soapy water from the tub and fill it with clear water to rinse the blinds. If the weather is warm you can take the blinds outside and hang them over the clothes line or a chair to dry. If not, stand them on end in the bathtub to drain most of the water, and then hang them back up at the window. Let them out full length until they are completely dry. If they have a lot of greasy dust on them, oh dear, I hope not—then you may have to use a soft brush to scrub them clean again while they are taking their "bath".

While your curtains or blinds are being cleaned, take the opportunity to wipe off any dust or cobwebs around the window areas and give all the window(s) a thorough cleaning.

Skills for Yearly Cleaning

There are several chores that only need to be done once a year. Aunt Sophie chooses one of these to do along with her monthly cleaning chores. She keeps track of when she did them on her calendar, and that way she knows when to schedule them the next year. Every efficient keeper of the home needs her own calendar & notebook. For a useful project, make your own "Home Notebook". Make the cover of your binder beautiful using your creative talents. Begin to fill it by adding these pages in it and add more pages of lists and calendar pages as you go along. Refer to it often to keep you "on track" at home.

- **Clean windows—inside & out**
- **Clean under the oven & refrigerator**
- **Clean window curtains and blinds**
- **Clean kitchen light fixtures**
- **Clean and organize the pantry**

Clean windows, inside and out:
Even though Aunt Sophie cleans her kitchen window pane on a regular basis, once a year she takes more time to clean both sides. She likes to choose a warm, sunny day for this pleasant task. You may have one piece windows, or you may have a window with a separate storm window. Learn how your windows work, and be sure you clean both the front and back of each pane of glass. Also, remove the screen and clean it with a vacuum cleaner attachment or take it out- side and spray it with the hose. Do this for all the windows in the kitchen area.

Clean under the oven and refrigerator:
This is one task where Aunt Sophie makes sure she asks for help! Get a strong helper to help move the refrigerator away from the wall. It will need to be moved as far out as the electric cord allows. Sweep the floor underneath, and then mop it. Use your vacuum cleaner attachment to vacuum the dust from the back of the refrigerator, making sure you also vacuum underneath the refrigerator from the back. Replace the refrigerator back where it belongs, and then follow the same instructions for cleaning under the stove.

Clean the kitchen light fixture(s):
Learn how your kitchen light is put together. Some lights are long fluorescent tubes with a removable plastic cover. Some are small lights placed at intervals around the wall of the room. What ever kind of light fixture you have, it probably has some kind of cover that needs to be taken down, cleaned and replaced. Depending on what it is made of, you can use glass cleaner or all-purpose cleaner or just plain warm soapy water. Be sure to dry the cover thoroughly before you replace it and if you had to remove any small screws—that you take care not to lose them!

Clean and organize the pantry:

Not everyone has a pantry that is separate from the kitchen cupboards. Aunt Sophie has shelves in her basement where she keeps food that she has canned and extra supplies of staples. A well-stocked pantry is a boon to the family kitchen. Having basic supplies on hand and only having to shop for necessities is a great time saver. If there is a separate pantry, it needs to be cleaned out once a year. Aunt Sophie has found that just before the summer canning season starts is a great time to get her pantry cleaned and tidy.

To clean the pantry:

First, clean off each shelf one at a time. Once the shelf is empty, wash and dry it. Now you can replace the items. Be sure to place the oldest items closest to the front of the shelf so they can be used first. Go through each of the shelves this way, examining all of your stored food as you go. If you have home canned foods on the shelf check each jar carefully to make sure the seal is still air tight. Look at the food inside the jar, and if it looks discolored or "funny" in any way, discard it in a receptacle where no pets can get into it.
Look carefully at each type of food you have stored, watching for any signs of bugs, mice droppings, or other vermin. Also look for any mold or damp packages that would indicate that your storage area is too damp. If you find any of these spoilers in your pantry take steps to fix it. Pantry moth traps can be changed out to new ones and some take precautions and keep mouse traps set out of the way in dark corners of a pantry.

"No-Nos" for Cooks

■ Never pick up any food off the floor and then serve it or eat it—anything dropped by accident must be discarded.

■ Never put any greasy liquids down the kitchen sink drain. They will clog and make trouble for the drains and septic systems.

■ Never cut raw meat on a cutting board and then use it without washing to cut other items like onions and such. Always wash it in very hot water with a good soap and then dry thoroughly.

■ Never use a fork or metal utensil to remove toast from a toaster! It must always be un plugged from the current before trying to remove a stuck piece of toast!

■ Never connect a plug into the electrical outlet with wet hands!

■ Never use any canned food that has bulging ends on the tin can. Food inside is most probably spoiled and harmful! Do not open it but discard it immediately in the garbage.

Family Table Courtesy

Sit properly at the table, sitting up straight
with your feet and legs under the table.

Sit quietly and politely until the food is served
or you are told to prepare your plate.

Place the napkin that is by your plate in your lap;
use it to wipe your mouth and hands.

Do not reach over others to get food.
Ask politely and someone nearby will pass it to you.

Happily eat the food that has been prepared
and do not ask for other foods not on the table.

Chew with your mouth closed and
do not talk while your mouth is full of food.

Mealtime conversations need to be appropriate table talk.

Do not take the last portion of food,
until offering it first to the others at the table.

Wait for all to finish their meal before asking about desserts.

Remember to thank the cook for the good meal.

Do not leave the table until you have been excused by the hostess or host.

Offer to help clean up the table after the meal, if you are able.

" Whether therefore ye eat, or drink, or whatsoever ye do, do all to the glory of God."
I Corinthians 10:31 KJV

"Blessed are they which do hunger and thirst after righteousness: for they shall be filled."
Matthew 5:6 KJV

Cookery Skills Checklist

I have learned the basic methods in cookery to:

___ Bake yeast rolls
___ Steam vegetables
___ Prepare a fresh green salad
___ Make a sandwich
___ Prepare oatmeal or porridge
___ Make toast
___ Cook omelets
___ Make pancakes
___ Make gravy
___ Make mashed potatoes
___ Cook scrambled eggs
___ Boil eggs
___ Cook rice
___ Make coffee and tea
___ Cook pasta
___ Make chicken or beef stock (broth)
___ Bake biscuits
___ Make and bake muffins from scratch
___ Learn to dice and chop onions
___ Learn to bake potatoes in the oven
___ Bake quick bread (cornbread or sweet banana bread)
___ Learn to cut up a whole chicken into parts
___ Roast a hen or turkey
___ Bake simple cookies from a recipe
___ Bake a cake from scratch
___ Make a basic white sauce (cream sauce)
___ Make 1 simple lunch menu to serve to 2
___ Make 2 simple breakfast menus to serve to 2-4
___Make 4 basic supper menus on my own to serve the family
___ Make 1 cake or sweet dessert

NAME: _____
has achieved the basic cookery skills listed above and has proven herself a
practical good cook.

Signed:

Mother Dear

Cookery Terms Mix & Match

Match the correct term with the correct definition. You will have to do some studying from other sources to find the answers if you are not familiar with these terms. In cooking terms, "fold" does not mean arrange your brother's shirt into a neat square for his dresser drawer, and "dust" does not mean to swipe the coffee table until it shines with a dusting cloth! So study up and learn these terms so you will be able to follow recipes and understand the procedures required.*The ANSWER KEY is found on the last page in this section!*

Bake: ____

Beat: ____

Blanch: ____

Blend: ____

Boil: ____

Brown: ____

Chill: ____

Coat: ____

Combine: ____

Cool: ____

Cream: ____

Cut in: ____

Dice: ____

Dot: ____

Dredge: ____

Dust: ____

Flour: ____

Fold: ____

Pan-fry: ____

Garnish: ____

Glaze: ____

Grate: ____

Grease: ____

Grind: ____

Knead: ____

Marinate: ____

Melt: ____

Mince: ____

Mix: ____

Mold: ____

Pare: ____

Peel: ____

Preheat: ____

Sauté: ____

Season: ____

Shred: ____

Sift: ____

Simmer: ____

Steep: ____

Stir: ____

Stock: ____

Toast: ____

Toss: ____

Whip: ____

[A] Cut food into small pieces—cube shaped.

[B] To heat food changing it from solid to liquid.

[C] Cut off the outer covering with a knife.

[D] Sprinkle food lightly with flour or sugar.

[E] To cook in a small amount of oil.

[F] To rub lightly with butter, oil, or shortening.

[G] Brown the surface using direct heat like a broiler or toaster oven.

[H] To put through a sieve or sifter to make finer or remove lumps.

[I] Brown in a small amount of hot fat (usually butter or oil).

[J] To extract flavor by pouring hot water over and letting stand without heating again.

[K] Beat rapidly with a mixer or whisk to incorporate air into the food and expand it.

[L] Tear or cut food into long, narrow pieces with a knife, hands or shedder.

[M] Combine by stirring until evenly distributed.

[N] Remove from heat and stand at room temperature until heat subsides.

[O] Cook a food until the surface is brown.

[P] Place in the refrigerator to bring to a cold temperature.

[Q] To make a mixture smooth by lifting it over and over using a mixer or spoon.

[R] To beat shortenings or butters until they are creamy smooth.

[S] Cover or sprinkle lightly with flour. (like chicken pieces)

[T] Mix together with a spoon or fork, moving it around until all combined and blended.

[U] Work dough with your hands, folding and stretching until it is smooth & elastic.

[V] Chop food very fine with a chopper or sharp knife.

[W] Strip off the outer covering of a fruit (like bananas or oranges).

[X] Mix lightly with two forks, with a lifting motion (like salad greens).

[Y] Combine 2 ingredients gently turning the mixture over & over with a rubber spatula.

[Z] To decorate foods with another colorful edible items (for eye appeal).

[AA] To cook in liquid just below boiling point.

[BB] To form into a shape.

[CC] To improve flavor of foods with salt, pepper, herbs or spice mixtures.

[DD] The liquid remaining from roasting or cooking meats, fish, vegetables or poultry.

[EE] To let food stand in a mixture for a period of time-tenderizes and absorbs flavor.

[FF] To cook with dry heat in an oven.

[GG] Heat the oven to a specific temperature before putting food in it.

[HH] To cook in liquid where bubbles constantly rise to the surface.

[II] To cover food in sugar, flour or crumbs by shaking in a bag or rolling in a mixture.

[JJ] Make a food into particles by rubbing over a sharp grater.

[KK] To mash or crush food by putting thru a meat grinder or processor.

[LL] To incorporate shortening into flour until it resembles small pea-like pieces.

[MM] To pour boiling water over or to dip into boiling water rapidly and then remove.

[NN] Coating a food with a thin icing or sugary syrup during or after baking.

[OO] To scatter small pieces of butter or cheese over the surface of a food.

[PP] To coat with fine crumbs or flour mixture.

Kitchen Safety

■ Run water over a used match to make sure it is completely extinguished before throwing in a waste can.

■ Use the right size pot to have plenty of room to avoid food or liquids boiling over onto your stove top.

■ Lay sharp knives and peelers aside after using in a safe place away from the reach of little hands. Wash each of these separately and dry and put away.

■ When a skillet or oven catches fire, turn off the unit immediately and dump baking soda or salt at the base of the flame. Never put water on a oven or stove fire! Keep the soda or salt in a handy place and be sure you know where they are kept!

■ Keep a fire extinguisher in the kitchen in an accessible place and know how to use it!

■ When placing boiling liquids into any glass container—set it first on a plate in the event the glass should crack. Never put boiling liquids into a glass container that is chilled or cold.

■ Do not put glass baking dishes in a hot oven if they are chilled or have frozen food in them. Put them into the cold oven, turn it on and then let the oven warm up to temperature with the cold dish inside.

■ Do not place handles of pots directly over other stove burners that are turned on to heat up.

■ Carefully choose the knob for which burner you are turning on. Always turn off the burner before taking off the pot. Then you will not forget to turn it off after you have removed the pot or pan.

■ Avoid nasty steam burns! Always lift off the lid of a boiling pot away from you so the steam can escape on the other side away from your hands or face.

■ Wipe up any spills or broken glass as soon as the accident happens!

■ Handle pots and oven dishes with a well-fitted oven mitt or sturdy thick hot pads. Do not use damp or wet cloths or pads as the heat will go right through it and possibly burn your hands!

■ Use a sturdy stepping stool when reaching in high places. Always be careful when climbing and reaching into high places that you are sturdy on your feet and your stool is secure and level on the floor.

■ Use non-skid pads under any small rugs in the kitchen area. Rugs can be slippery and cause falls without the under pads.

Answer Key for Mix & Match Cookery Terms

Some terms are basically the same and use the same definition as in "T" - it is used up 3 times for "blend; combine; stir" —though each of these are a bit different you basically end up with the same result after doing any of them.

Bake: FF
Beat: Q
Blanch: MM
Blend: T
Boil: HH
Brown: O
Chill: P
Coat: II
Combine: T
Cool: N
Cream: R
Cut in: LL
Dice: A
Dot: OO
Dredge: PP
Dust: D
Flour: S
Fold: Y
Pan-fry: E
Garnish: Z
Glaze: NN
Grate: JJ
Grease: F
Grind: KK
Knead: U
Marinate: EE
Melt: B
Mince: V
Mix: M
Mold: BB
Pare: C
Peel: W
Preheat: GG
Sauté: I
Season: CC
Shred: L
Sift: H
Simmer: A A
Steep: J
Stir: T
Stock: DD
Toast: G
Toss: X
Whip: K

Suggested Recipes below for "Doubling or Downsizing" Project Assignment

Cookie recipes can be doubled easily—dough chilled and then molded into a log roll inside wax paper and the ends twisted up to seal. Drop into zipper baggies and when you want fresh baked cookies—take the dough logs from the freezer and thaw just slightly and slice into 1/2" thick slices and bake just as directed for cookies on the original recipe. Record/write your new measurement amounts in the { }.

Kari's Chocolate Chip Cookies

Beat together until fluffy and creamy:
{   } 1/2 cup sugar
{   } 1 cup brown sugar
{   } 3/4 cups soft butter (not melted!) Add in:
{   } 2 large fresh eggs Beat until combined.
Then add in the rest of the ingredients to follow and combine all just until all dry ingredients are incorporated.
{   } 2 1/2 cups plain all-purpose flour
{   } 1 teaspoon baking soda +
{   } 1 teaspoon salt +
{   } 1 teaspoon vanilla
Add in: 4 cups of chocolate chip pieces and stir until incorporated into the dough. Chill dough in refrigerator for up to 2 hours. Scoop or roll into 1" size balls and flatten just slightly and place on a lightly greased baking or cookie sheet. Bake in a preheated oven at 375 degrees for 9-11 minutes. Cookies should just be lightly browned around the edges. Remove from oven and let stand on baking sheet for 10 minutes before removing to a wire rack to cool.

Big batch granola recipes can easily be down-sized to make a smaller amount. Record/write your new measurement amounts in the { }.

Poppee's Nut Butter Granola

Add these ingredients to a large saucepan and heat until all melted together—stirring frequently:
{   } 1/2 cup coconut oil (can substitute other oil)
{   } 2 cups brown sugar
{   } 2 cups crunchy style peanut butter
{   } 1/2 cup water
{   } 1/2 cup butter
{   } 3 teaspoons vanilla

Now put {   } 12 cups of rolled oats (uncooked oatmeal) into a very large bowl. Pour the hot peanut butter mixture over the oatmeal and mix with a large sturdy spoon until oats are all moist. Place this all into a large greased roaster pan and bake at 325 degrees for 20-30 minutes stirring once during baking. Cool and store the granola in a large snap lid container. Refrigeration is not needed. Serve in a bowl with fresh cold milk poured over and a sliced banana top. You can try it sprinkled on ice cream or yogurt too!

Lovely Living Areas

A Guide to the
Living Rooms of the Home

My dear girls ~

When we think of the living rooms of our homes, what do we think of?

These are places for our family to be together. They are places for play, conversation, hospitality, and worship. The important thing about a living area is not the room itself, but what happens in the room. The room is the container. Just as a lovely vase enhances a beautiful bouquet of flowers, a lovely living area enhances what a family does in it.

A wise homemaker carefully chooses furnishings, colors, and decorations to make the living area a vessel fit for her family. She spends time in the living areas to keep them clean and free of clutter, knowing that peaceful, orderly rooms are pleasing to be in. She also arranges the rooms so that each member of the family feels at home, with places for conversation, reading, and play.

I hope my girls will learn to love making their living areas into beautiful vases for their families.

— Aunt Sophie

Living Rooms
Home Skills Checklist

I can confidently keep house in the living room of the home by knowing the skills needed regarding:

___ How to pick up & put away

___ How to dust furniture

___ How to use a vacuum cleaner & do vacuuming

___ How to sweep with a broom and use a dust pan

___ How to make an arrangement of the room's furniture

___ How to make an accent pillow cover

___ How to repot a small plant

___ How to do a quick tidy-up of a living room in 15 minutes

NAME: _____ has passed the requirements for our home listed above and has proven herself a capable keeper of a home.

Signed:

MotherDear

Living Rooms
Home Skills Scheduling Chart

DAILY

Pick up and put away

Light Dusting

Vacuum or sweep floors

WEEKLY

Dust

Vacuum

Water houseplants

MONTHLY

Sort thru magazine and paper stacks

Dust and polish furniture

Vacuum couch & chair cushions

Clean under area rugs or shake & clean smaller rugs

SEASONALLY

Wash windows, blinds and curtains

Add and arrange décor to fit the season

Clean and rearrange books and bookshelves

YEARLY

Clean upholstered furniture and cushions

Re-pot houseplants

Clean carpeting and floors

Skills for Daily Cleaning

Just as she does in every other area of her home, Aunt Sophie has daily, weekly, monthly, seasonal, and yearly tasks in her living rooms. You may have only one living area, or you may have two or even three, depending on the size of your house and how your family uses it. It doesn't matter how many rooms you have as living areas, the idea is the same for all of them. These regular tasks help to keep these areas clean, orderly and ready for your family to use them.

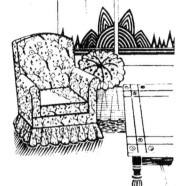

There are three items on Aunt Sophie's daily checklist for the living areas:

- **Pickup & put away**
- **Light dusting**
- **Vacuum**

Pick up & put away:

Aunt Sophie's rule for every area of her home is "a place for everything and everything in its place", but she knows that as her family uses their living areas, some things get out of their places, or new things are introduced. A new magazine may come in the mail, or the little ones play with toys and don't put them away. Quite often a book will be put down without being put away, or the music is left open on the piano. Aunt Sophie takes just a few minutes once a day to go through the living areas to make sure that everything is in its place.

Of course, this means that Aunt Sophie has already decided ahead of time where each thing belongs. When there are little ones living in the house, she makes sure that there is a basket to keep toys in. She has a special basket next to a chair where magazines go. There is a special place on the bookshelf for piano music, and another place on the bookshelf for books that are currently being read. Library books have their own basket, and there is a cupboard for the family's games. Having a place for everything is the first step in keeping your living areas clean and free of clutter.

Light dusting:

Aunt Sophie keeps a feather duster with her while she picks up and puts away the things in her living area, and while she goes around the room she quickly dusts the tables and shelves. In her daily dusting, Aunt Sophie doesn't move anything out of the way, but just makes sure there isn't any dust on those flat surfaces.

Vacuum:

The last thing Aunt Sophie does in her living areas each day is to quickly run the vacuum sweeper over the carpet. If you have a wood or linoleum floor, you can sweep the floor.

Skills for Weekly Cleaning

- Dust
- Vacuum
- Water house plants

Dust:

While doing her daily tasks, Aunt Sophie lightly dusts the flat surfaces as she picks up the room, but once a week she dusts everything in her living room. For this dusting Aunt Sophie uses a clean, soft cotton cloth that she sprays with a furniture spray before using. The furniture spray helps the cloth attract dust and also helps to pol- ish the wood furniture.

Vacuum:

In her weekly vacuuming, Aunt Sophie makes sure she moves her furniture and vacuums underneath. She works around the room in an orderly way. When she comes to a piece of furniture that can be moved, such as a chair, she first vacuums the floor in front of the chair. Then she moves the chair onto the vacuumed space and vacuums the area underneath and behind where the chair had been sitting. When she replaces the chair she makes sure that it is in a slightly different place than it was before – this is to keep from getting worn spots in the carpet where the chair's feet sit.

Water House Plants:

Aunt Sophie likes to keep a few house plants in her living room. They help to soften the room and bring a bit of life into it. Once a week, or every other week for the plants that don't need as much water, Aunt Sophie waters the plants. Be sure to keep saucers under the plants so that the excess water doesn't go on your furniture or floors!

"You won't see the daisy in the budvase
if there is a dirty sock in the middle of the floor!"

How to Dust

Dust in an orderly fashion: start at one spot in the room and move around the room clockwise, dusting everything you come to. Work from top to bottom as you dust. Shake your cloth or duster out regularly. Be sure to shake it outside so that the dust is removed from your room! While you're dusting, don't forget the hard to reach places. Picture frames and knick-knacks on high shelves are often overlooked. When you come to lamps, knick-knacks or other objects on the shelves or tables, be sure to dust them, then pick them up and dust underneath them.

Tools for Dusting

Vacuum Cleaner:

Your vacuum cleaner is a great tool for dusting. Use the wand with various attachments to dust rough surfaces, like the bricks around a fireplace. Another attachment is made for dusting cloth draperies and upholstered furniture. An attachment called a crevice tool works well to clean in between couch cushions and along the base-boards of your walls.

Dusters:

These may be made of feathers, lambs wool, or may be a commercial product. Some, like feather dusters, rely on many tiny filaments to trap dust. Others, like commercial products you can buy, rely on an electrostatic charge (static electricity) to attract and trap dust. Dusters are good for dusting things with small crevices and to give a quick dusting where needed. When buying a duster, remember that quality makes all the difference. A cheap feather duster will do no more than push the dust around. A thrifty housekeeper invests in a quality product that will last for years.

Dust cloths:

These can be anything from an old cotton t-shirt or sock to a microfiber dust cloth that you buy at the store. You can even buy some that are pre-treated with dusting spray. Dust cloths are great for dusting objects and the surfaces underneath them. It is a good idea to wash your dust cloth every week so that you have a clean one to use every time you dust. Furniture polish or spray: Most furniture polish only needs to be used once in awhile. Be sure to read the instructions so that you know how to use them and what surfaces they are used on. There are other products that are made specifically for dusting. They are sprays that you can spray on your dust cloth to help it pick up dust more easily. Again, be sure to read the instructions on the product.

Furniture polish or spray:

Most furniture polish only needs to be used once in awhile. Be sure to read the instructions so that you know how to use them and what surfaces they are used on. There are other products that are made specifically for dusting. They are sprays that you can spray on your dust cloth to help it pick up dust more easily. Again, be sure to read the instructions on the product.

The Furnishings

Your home may have a formal living room as well as a family room or den, which would be much less formal. If your home has only one living area then it should be a combination of beauty and comfort. There are many elements to use in furnishing your living areas to make them into the right spaces for your family to use and to give them a comfortable, lovely feeling.

Seating:

It is important for your room to have enough seating so that when family or friends gather everyone can be seated comfortably. Living rooms also need comfortable furniture, and a variety of different types. There is usually a sofa (that seats up to three people) and/or a love seat (that seats up to two people), and quite often one or two upholstered chairs that coordinate with the sofa. These large upholstered items form the main framework of your furniture. Other furniture for seating may include one or two smaller occasional chairs, perhaps a rocking chair, and footstools or ottomans that can double as seating. The arrangement of the furniture depends on your living room – its size and shape, and how many doors and windows you need to take into consideration – but it is important to keep the room's purpose in mind when placing the furniture.

A fun way to decide how to arrange the furniture in your room is to try out different ideas on paper. Aunt Sophie likes to use paper cut outs to represent her different pieces of furniture and then draws a representation of her room on graph paper. It is very important to measure the room and each piece of furniture so that you have an accurate model to use. With these tools Aunt Sophie can try out different ways of arranging her furniture so that it uses the space in her room the best way.

It is tempting, especially if your room is small, to line the furniture up against the wall. However, Aunt Sophie has discovered that it is hard for people to make conversation if the room is too formal and regimented. She has learned to place the furniture around a central point in the room, keeping enough distance between the furniture to keep the room from feeling crowded. When a chair is placed at an angle to a sofa, then all of the people sitting on those pieces of furniture can see each other while they talk. Other things to take into consideration when placing furniture is traffic flow – does your room have two or more doors or entryways? Then you need to place the furniture so that people can walk easily from one entry to another.

One thing Aunt Sophie decided many years ago is that her living room is not as large as the crowds of family and friends she would like to see in it! It is impossible to have enough seating space for everyone, so she came up with a solution. Her living room has enough seating for her family, but she keeps folding chairs on hand in a nearby closet to bring out when friends come over. These small chairs can fit easily into the spaces between the other furniture and everyone can have a place to sit.

Other furniture:

Along with places for people to sit in your living room, you may also have side tables and perhaps a coffee table. Other pieces may include bookshelves or an armoire (a large, ornate cabinet, often with shelves and drawers) or a piano. These items can be placed against the walls, but be aware of how easily they can be accessed. The side tables can be placed next to the main seating to provide a place for a lamp and to set a book down. The coffee table, if you have one, is usually placed in front of the sofa. It can be used to display books or magazines, or can be used as a focal point for the room.

Lighting:

The best lighting in a living room is a combination of general area lighting and reading lamps. Overhead lighting is good for work areas like kitchens, but can seem harsh and overpowering in a living room. The most effective way to light a living room is to have lighting on two different levels. Think of the vertical space in your room as having three layers. The top third of the room is what you see at eye level when you are standing up, the middle third is at eye level when you are sitting down, and the bottom third is from the seating level down to the floor. Depending on the size of your room, it works well to have two or three lamps in both the upper and middle layers. For the upper layer of lighting floor lamps work well, or perhaps your room has lights in the ceiling or sconces on the walls that illuminate the top third of the wall. Any of these solutions work well to provide light for the top layer. For the middle layer table lamps work well. Lamps that provide enough light to read by as a person is sitting in one of the chairs or sofa is ideal.

Another thing to consider when choosing lighting for your room is that the lamp shades and styles of lamps are a large part of the visual atmosphere of your room. Lamps don't need to match each other in color and style, but they should coordinate. Be careful to choose colors that compliment your furniture.

Music:

Whether your source of music is live (a piano or other instrument) or electronic (a CD player, for example), music adds an element to your living area that can't be achieved any other way. Music lends peace and harmony to the atmosphere and can set the mood for your room. Music can be the family singing to- gether, a family member playing an instrument for the rest of the family, a recording of sacred or praise music, or your family's favorite music playing in the background during a family game. As you think about furnishing your living room, think about where you can add music. It can be as simple as a small CD player on a shelf, or as ornate as a grand piano gracing one end of the room.

Walls:

The final piece to your living area is the wall space. Think of the wall space in the room as the background to the activities, and choose what you place on them carefully. Hanging something on the wall just to fill a bare spot doesn't add to the atmosphere of the room, but placing a favorite picture or arrangement of family photographs reinforces the room's hominess. A group of small items on one wall can make a pleasing contrast to a large picture on another wall. Personal items such as needlework done by a family member or mementoes of shared family times can also be meaningful decorations. Your goal in this room is to provide a place for your family to be together and your choices will reflect that

Advice on Flowers & Ornaments in the Living Area from Grandmother Foster:

"All bowls, vases and jugs used for flowers need to be cleaned frequently or the decaying leaves and stems will cause a bad odor; besides, clear glass ornaments show the sediment inside. The finest cut glass vase it not attractive unless it is clean, and after being brushed in the warm suds and washed inside with a cloth, it can be rinsed in clear water and left to drain dry."

"Everyone likes to see pretty things about the living-room, and my girls will all be interested in learning the right way to care for bric-a-brac, books, music and pictures. Nothing detracts from their beauty so much as dust and finger marks, and it requires some experience to handle and keep them clean. Vases, statuettes, and ornaments of all kinds should be examined on every sweeping day. Dust them with a soft cloth or a little brush, and the pieces that need washing remove to the kitchen. The other can be set in another room or covered on a table while the rooms are being cleaned, and then carefully replaced. The pieces that need washing should be put in a basin or warm soapsuds, and scrubbed gen- tly with a nail-brush or a small, fine bristle brush such as artists use, but first be sure that the decorations will not wash off of delicate things."

Excerpted from Housekeeping for Little Girls by Olive H. Foster circa 1922

Skills for Monthly Cleaning

- Sort through magazines and paper stacks
- Vacuum couch & chair cushions
- Clean & polish wood furniture
- Clean under area rugs or shake & clean smaller rugs

Sort through magazines and paper stacks:

If your family subscribes to any magazines, then you know that a new magazine comes in the mail every month or two. Your family may also receive catalogs in the mail that are saved until the new one comes out. Aunt Sophie knows that if she doesn't sort through these on a regular basis they can pile up quickly. So once a month she sorts through the magazines and catalogs that have accumulated. Many of these, especially the catalogs, can just be taken to the recycling or trash bin. Some magazines have patterns or recipes that Aunt Sophie wants to save. If these things are on only one or two pages, she cuts them out of the magazine and puts them in a notebook, and then disposes of the rest of the magazine. There are a couple magazines that Aunt Sophie saves to refer to later and she has a special place on her bookshelf for these. The goal at the end of the sorting is to have only the most recent copy of a magazine or catalog in the magazine basket. This is also a good time to make sure that any library books that are close to their due date are ready to be returned to the library.

Vacuum couch and chair cushions:

Once a month Aunt Sophie uses her vacuum cleaner attachments to clean her upholstered furniture. Most vacuum cleaners have an upholstery tool – a small flat piece with very short bristles on it – and a crevice tool. Both are used to clean upholstered furniture. First, if the cushions on the furniture are removable, take them off one by one and vacuum them using the upholstery tool. This will remove any dust and dirt that has seeped into the fabric. Then, using the upholstery tool, vacuum all of the remaining surfaces of the piece of furniture. And last, use the crevice tool to vacuum the spaces where the backs and sides of the furniture meet the bottom.

Clean and polish wood furniture:

If you have wood furniture, it needs to be cared for to preserve the wood and keep it looking nice. Aunt Sophie polishes her wood tables and piano once a month. There are many commercial furniture polishes available.

Clean under area rugs or shake and clean smaller rugs:

An old time saying is well-known "They sweep it under the rug" meaning that instead of confronting or facing a problem—they just hide it or ignore it. If you lift up a large area rug in a living room— you may be surprised to find what is hiding under there! Rugs are made to catch dirt and so they need to be rolled up and cleaned under with a vacuum or broom on a regular basis. Small area rugs that are washable can be given a thorough shake out of doors —or your grandmother probably hung it over the fence or clothesline and beat all the dust and dirt out of it. Some smaller rugs are washable and can be washed or hosed down and then hung out to dry.

Skills for Seasonal Cleaning

- Wash windows, blinds and curtains
- Clean and rearrange books and bookshelves
- Arrange and add seasonal décor

How to wash windows:

Aunt Sophie loves to see the sun streaming through her living room windows, but it can be very disheartening if the sun shining through shows how dirty those windows are! To keep your windows sparkling clean, it's important to wash them on a regular basis. Use the same tools that you use for windows and mirrors in other parts of the house – Aunt Sophie uses glass cleaner and old newspapers to make her windows sparkle. She chooses a sunny day for this task so that she can see the fruit of her labors right away.

Before cleaning your windows, it's important to know how your windows are constructed. Find out what kind of windows your house has and how to dismantle them for cleaning. You may have a one piece window with double or triple panes sealed in the frame. These windows are easy to clean, and only need to be washed on the inside and outside sur- faces. Sometimes these windows can tilt into the house, which makes cleaning even eas- ier. If you have an older house, or if the windows haven't been replaced recently, you may have separate storm windows. These will need to be taken apart and each pane cleaned separately. With either style of window, take time to vacuum the screen before replacing everything.

About window treatments:

The blinds or curtains you have at your windows are called window treatments. There are four different kinds, and all four need to be cleaned in a different way. If you have blinds (sometimes called mini-blinds or Venetian blinds), either metal or plastic, they can be taken down and washed. Aunt Sophie has found that the easiest way to wash them is in the bathtub! Run water in your bathtub to a depth of about three inches, adding dishwashing soap to the water. One window at a time, remove the blinds from the windows. Extend them to their longest length (to separate the slats) and gently place them in the water. Swish them around in the water a few times, being careful not to tan- gle the lines, and then let them soak. After about 30 minutes, swish them around again and check to see if the dirt is coming off the slats. If not, you may need to use a soft bris- tled brush or a cloth to scrub each slat. When the blinds are clean, rinse them off and hang them up to dry. On nice days you can hang them over the clothes line, and in bad weather you can use the shower curtain rod over the bathtub. Once the blinds have drip- dried replace them on the window.

Another kind of window treatment you may have is window shades. These are solid vinyl or cloth shades that roll up at the top of the window. The window shades should be vacuumed to clean them, or if a vinyl shade is very dirty it can be washed. To wash it, take the shade down from the window and roll it out on a clean, flat surface (a long table or a clear space on the floor). Fill a bucket with warm, soapy water and use a clean cloth. Starting at one end of the shade, wipe the shade clean using the damp cloth and soapy water. Once one side of the shade is clean, wipe it off with a dry cloth, then flip it over and wash and dry the other side. Before re-rolling and hanging the shade make sure it is thoroughly dry, or else mildew may form on it!

The third and fourth kinds of window treatments are curtains and drapes. What is the difference? Aunt Sophie usually calls window treatments made of cloth or lace curtains if they are made of a material that can be washed and draperies if the material can't be washed! Curtains are usually lighter weight and often cover only part of a window. Draperies are heavier in weight and usually cover the entire window, although they may also only frame a window without being able to be closed.

Washing curtains:
To wash curtains, remove them from the curtain rods and put them in your washing machine set on a gentle cycle. Either dry them in the dryer or hang them to dry. Once they are dry, give them a light pressing with the iron and they are ready to re-hang. Draperies should not be washed in the washing machine. To keep them clean, vacuum them often (during your weekly cleaning). If they need to be cleaned more thoroughly, take them to a professional cleaner.

There are many other styles of window treatments which haven't been covered here. In general, if the material your window treatment is made of is able to be washed, then use mild soap and water. If it isn't washable, then use your vacuum attachment often to keep it clean.

Sort through bookshelves:
Every few months it's time to purge the bookshelves in the living areas. Aunt Sophie loves to read and if she's not careful, the books and magazines will fill her house! So she takes time to go through the bookshelves and takes out books that she has read and en- joyed. Some she passes on to friends that she knows will enjoy them and some she donates to the local used book sale. After removing the extra books, she thoroughly cleans and rearranges the shelves. If your living room accommodates furniture that has cabinets, treat them the same way you would the open shelves. Take out the items stashed inside those cabinets. Sort thru, tidy up, dust and clean off the shelves inside the cabinets and put everything back neatly. If there is a lot of clutter inside—take the time to sort it and discard or give away what is no longer of use to you and your household.

Home Decorator Tip:

It gives a pleasing look to vary the items on your open book shelves. Size and group books according to subjects and size. Lay some books on their sides instead of upright for a variance in design. Place some smaller well-loved books in a pretty decorative box. Every so often perch a basket or ornamental object on the shelves to break up the "soldier" line of book upon book. Place a pretty framed print or family photograph randomly on various shelves.

Arrange and add seasonal decorations:

Aunt Sophie loves the change of seasons! She has a few decorations that she changes with each season and they help keep the living areas looking fresh and new. To help things look pretty, it's important to choose your decorations so that the colors comple- ment each other and your room. Using objects that mean something to your family is also important – after all, this room is for them and is your home—not a showcase gallery in a furniture store.

Spring Ideas:

A decorative bird house on a shelf can be pretty, and fresh flowers are a welcome change from winter. Aunt Sophie uses silk ivy on her top bookshelf to soften that area, and has pretty spring pillows to put on the couch.

Summer Ideas:

Aunt Sophie's summer decorations have a beach feel to them. She uses sea shells in a basket, and a cute wooden sailboat is on the shelf where the birdhouse was in the spring. She found a fish net at a craft store and drapes that on the top shelf. A couple whimsical sea gulls stand on top of the piano. The Spring pillows on the couch are replaced with new covers in perky Summer fabric. Choose a theme or idea that says "Summer" to you. It could be red gingham pillow covers & blooming red geraniums in a large pots stretched across the fireplace hearth. (The fireplace won't be used for the Summer months). Whatever you like and will have the feel of "cool & comfortable" to you—give your living room a change!

Autumn Ideas:

The decorations for autumn can have a harvest theme. Aunt Sophie uses a basket to display gourds, and scatters silk autumn leaves on the piano. A ceramic pilgrim couple is on the top shelf and an autumn scented candle is on the mantle. Aunt Sophie made an afghan from colors of yarn that match the autumn pillows on the couch, and that is kept conveniently on the back of a chair.

Winter Ideas:

Aunt Sophie's winter decorations are a backdrop to the Christmas decorations. She has some wooden pine trees that go on the shelf, and winter greenery on the top of the bookshelf. She also puts a string of white lights behind the greenery to give some extra light in the room on dark evenings. The candle on the mantle is replaced with a pine scented one, and the winter pillows and matching afghan are on the couch. During Advent and the Christmas season Aunt Sophie adds her family's favorite Christmas items to the living areas, and when they are put away at the end of the holiday the winter decorations stay until spring.

Skills for Yearly Cleaning

- **Clean carpeting and floors**
- **Clean upholstered furniture**
- **Repot houseplants**

Clean carpeting and floors:

Even with regular vacuuming the carpeting in Aunt Sophie's house can get very dirty, so once a year she shampoos her carpets. Aunt Sophie owns a carpet shampooer and appreciates having this tool. Shampooers are also available to rent at some grocery and hardware stores. Be sure to buy the kind of shampoo that the machine you use recommends. Pre-treating sprays are also available and help in high traffic areas where the carpet can get very dirty.

Before starting to clean the carpet in a room, remove as many pieces of furniture as you can. Heavy items, like a piano or bookcases, can be left in place. Vacuum the carpet thoroughly. Pre-treat any spots or obviously dirty areas with a pre-treating spray, and then shampoo the carpet. Be sure to carefully follow the directions on the machine you are using.

After you are done shampooing the carpet, go back and get as much of the shampoo out of the carpet as you can using the "rinse" setting on the machine. Next, go back over the carpeting again with just the vacuum setting on the machine. This will get as much of the water out of the carpet as possible. Let your carpet dry thoroughly before replacing the furniture. If you need to put the furniture back in the room before the carpet is completely dry, place small pieces of aluminum foil under the furniture legs to keep them from discoloring the damp carpet.

If you have hardwood floors instead of carpeting, then they will not need a yearly cleaning. Instead, keep them clean with daily and weekly sweeping and damp mop them weekly using a gallon of warm water with one cup of vinegar. Water isn't good for wood floors, so make sure your mop is almost dry when mopping the floor. Once every five to seven years your floor may need heavier treatment, but consult the manufacturer of your floor for specifics.

Clean upholstered furniture:

One thing Aunt Sophie has learned about upholstered furniture is that some furniture can be cleaned with the upholstery attachment on the carpet shampooer, and other kinds need to be treated differently. The first thing to do is to look at the manufacturer's label on your furniture. You can usually find this under the cushions or on the underside of your furniture. Look for the manufacturer's code that tells you how to clean this item:

• If there is a W you can use water based cleaner. You can spot clean the upholstery using the foam only of a mild detergent or the upholstery attachment of your carpet shampooer. Don't use too much, and avoid getting the furniture too wet.

• If there is an S then you need to use a water-free dry cleaning solvent. This is available in stores. Use it sparingly, and make sure the room is well ventilated. As when using any commercial product, read and follow the directions carefully.

• If there is an S-W then you can use either a water-based or a solvent cleaner. Choose which cleaner to use depending on the stain – mud or most foods can be cleaned with a water-based cleaner, and any stain with grease will need a solvent cleaner. Spot clean the fabric.

• If there is an X it means that you can only use a vacuum or a light brushing to clean this fabric. Any other kinds of cleaners will ruin the fabric.

• Aunt Sophie has learned to look for these codes on furniture before she makes a new purchase. She always tries to buy the fabrics that are easiest to clean – the ones with "W" or "S-W" codes.

Repot house plants:

This is one chore that Aunt Sophie loves to do on a warm autumn day. She puts many of her house plants outside during the summer months, and before bringing them into the house for the winter they need to be cleaned, thinned and, every two or three years, repotted.

Before starting it's a good idea to have all of your supplies handy. Each plant that you are repotting will need a pot that is slightly larger than the one it is currently in. Plan carefully so that you can reuse pots as you go. You will also need a bag of potting soil, a trowel, gardening gloves, and newspaper.

Spread the newspaper out on your working surface – a picnic table works well if you don't have a potting bench. If the weather isn't cooperative you can also do this chore at the kitchen table or counter – just be sure to use plenty of newspaper to keep the surface clean and clean up thoroughly when you're done!

Place each plant on your work surface and examine it carefully. Look at the stems and undersides of the leaves to check for any bugs or other problems. If needed, treat the plant with spray according to the directions on the bottle. Some plants, especially if they have broad leaves, can look so much better if you wipe each leaf with a damp cloth to clean off dirt and dust. Thin out any excess growth or dead growth and trim back overgrown branches or vines. If the plant hasn't been repotted for a few years, then this is a good time to do it.

For each plant that you are repotting, remove it carefully from its pot. Check the roots to see if the plant is root bound. A root bound plant will have roots showing on the outside of the dirt, and if it is severely root bound, the roots will be thick and dis- colored. You should remove any roots that are not a bright white color, and loosen the remaining roots. Don't be alarmed if some of the roots get damaged - they will heal, and it is important to only have the healthy growing roots in your new pot. Put new potting soil in the bottom inch or so of the new pot and place the plant in. Fill in soil around the plant, packing it in (but not too firmly). Water the plant thoroughly. If your plant was severely root bound it may take a few months to recover from this treatment, but it will be much healthier in the long run.

Courtesies for Company

Wipe your shoes thoroughly before entering inside from outside.
♥

A gentleman always stands when a lady enters the room.
♥

A gentleman will always defer a seat to the ladies
if there is not enough seating.
♥

If adults are having a conversation, children should play or talk quietly and not
interrupt, except for an emergency.
♥

It is not courteous to have the television on
while company is in the living room.
♥

The radio should be turned off to give your full attention to the guests.
♥

Keep your feet off the furniture and sit properly.
♥

OUR HOME GROWS

TENDER PLANTS

Provident Pantries

A Guide to
Stocking & Using a
Home Pantry

My dear girls ~

I hope you've learned the lesson of the ant from the Bible:

"Go to the ant, thou sluggard; consider her ways and be wise: which having no guide, overseer, or ruler, provideth her meat in the summer, and gathereth her food in the harvest."
Proverbs 6:6-8 [KJV]

A well-stocked pantry is what helps us live out that lesson. A wise home maker knows the needs of her household, obtains the items that are needed when they are plentiful, stores them well so that they are ready when needed rather than spoiled, and uses the items she stores.

My pantry is such an important part of managing my home that I can't imagine not having one. Through these pages you'll learn about the ins and outs of building, maintaining, and using a pantry. Learning about this important homemaking skill will give you, as a girl still at home, knowledge that will be of untold value when you begin to manage your own home.

~ Aunt Sophie

The Pantry
Home Skills Checklist

I can confidently feed those who I am responsible for by knowing the skills needed in the home regarding:

___ How to start a pantry

___ How to organize a pantry

___ How to stock a pantry

___ How to use foods from the pantry

___ How to clean and keep a pantry

NAME:

_____

has passed the requirements for our home listed above and has proven herself a capable keeper of a home.

Signed:

MotherDear

What is a Pantry?

A pantry is a collection of stored supplies of food and household items needed to keep the home running smoothly. These items are kept available for the family to use when needed. Many people think of a pantry as only containing food, but Aunt Sophie's pantry is much more than that! Her pantry contains food, of course, but also paper products, cleaning sup- plies, personal products and any other miscellaneous items that are used in her home.

Pantries have an interesting history. The idea of the pantry started in late-Medieval times. In the castles and great halls of those times there were separate rooms to store and prepare the different kinds of food. The pantry was where bread was kept and prepared, and the person responsible for this room was called the "pantler". The word "pantry" is derived from the French word for bread, *"pain"* (pronounced "pan"). In Colonial America, pantries started out as a "butt'ry" – a room in the coldest part of the house (usually the north-east corner) – and evolved into the more general pantry and root cellar on self-sufficient farmsteads. In middle-class homes of the Victorian era, the pantry became a room between the kitchen and dining room that acted to separate the two rooms. Plates, dishes and utensils were kept there, and there was usually a sink to wash the dishes.

Our pantries today can look very different from one home to the next. Some houses have basements with plenty of storage space, and a pantry works well on shelves in a corner. Some houses have a closet with shelves in it just off the kitchen. Other homes have very little storage space, and the prudent homemaker becomes very creative in where to store her pantry items! For today's homemaker, a pantry refers more to what is stored than a separate room.

A wise homemaker stores what she uses,

and uses what she stores.

Why Have a Pantry?

One of Aunt Sophie's models for homemaking is the woman of Proverbs 31. In verse 21 of that chapter we read that "she is not afraid of the snow for her household," because she is prepared. Before winter comes she has prepared warm clothes for her family (vs. 21), she gardens and provides food for her family (vs. 15 and 16), and she is diligent in her work (vs. 27). She has prepared for the snow – for the hard times ahead.

Even if you don't live where snow storms can keep you from leaving your home for days at a time, every family needs to be prepared for hard times. Your family may have experienced times when a storm has knocked out your electricity, or a hurricane has made it impossible to get to the store. Perhaps your family has experienced months when there has been no money coming into the home because of job loss or illness. A well-stocked pantry is the homemaker's best friend for hard times!

A well-stocked pantry also saves money. Aunt Sophie replenishes her pantry when the items she uses are plentiful or on sale. She also saves time, money and gas by making regular monthly trips to the store rather than weekly. A prudent homemaker plans her purchases and uses her money wisely – buying for the future instead of for the present need makes that possible.

A word about thrift from Grandmother Foster

"You would not think of throwing away a quarter, would you? I see you open your eyes in astonishment. But if you do not "run the house" on what is called a business basis, you will throw away (waste) a good many quarters! Every girl should take pride in learning how to get the most for her money, and saving all she can. In the first place, she should know exactly how much she has to spend, then just exactly what she needs to buy. Here will come in the fun of seeing how far she can make the money go."

Excerpted from Housekeeping for Little Girls by Olive H. Foster circa ❖ 1922

How to Start a Pantry

If your family doesn't already have a pantry, then starting one can seem like a daunting task! But if you break that task down into smaller steps, then it will be easier.

The first thing to do is to sit down with your mother and make a list of all the items – food and non-food – that your family uses in a month. Work through the items by categories: canned goods, baking items, grains (cereals, pastas), beans (dried and canned), paper products such as bathroom tissue and paper towels, personal hygiene products such as toothpaste and shampoo…there are many, many items to consider, and after you make your first list, you'll find yourself adding to it as you remember things that you've forgotten. You can refer to the sample list in this lesson for ideas, but it is very important that your list contains the items *your* family uses!

As you're making your list, estimate the quantities of each item that your family will use in one month. For some things, like spices, one container may last several months, and you can estimate a quantity like "1/6" if you think that item may last for six months. One of the jobs of the prudent homemaker is to constantly revise those quantities as needed.

Next, take an inventory of what you already have on hand. Even if you've never had a pantry before, you probably have most of the items on your list already – after all, they are things your family uses! With your mother, decide how many of each item you will need to buy to provide a one month supply for your family, and then use your next few shopping trips (as your grocery budget will allow) to bring the amounts of your pantry items up to your one month goal.

Once you have your pantry stocked for one month, you can increase the amounts of each item to a new goal – perhaps your family's next goal will be a three month supply. Multiply the amounts on your list by three, and work to supply your pantry to those levels. Aunt Sophie's pantry has a one year supply of goods for her family.

At the same time that you'll be stocking your pantry, you're also going to be using items from it. Make it a habit to keep a list of what you take out of your pantry to use for meals and family needs. If you write down each thing as you remove it, then you know what you will need to replenish on your next shopping trip.

Another habit to develop is to read your store sale fliers each week. As things that you use come on sale you can stock up. If canned tomatoes are on your list, and your store has a sale on them, you can stock up on tomatoes for your pantry by as much as your budget will allow. In this case, don't worry about buying more than the quantity on your list – the items will keep and you'll save money in the long run. Just don't worry about replenishing the supply of canned tomatoes until the quantity in your storage drops down toward the minimum number that you want to have on hand.

As we mentioned earlier, each house will have a different size and type of storage space available. An ideal pantry would have shelves located in a cool, dark area of the house, such as a basement, a room next to the garage, or even space in the garage (if it is insulated so that it doesn't freeze). You should also include freezer space in your thinking, since many meats, fruits and vegetables can be frozen. A small chest freezer is large enough for most families (unless you raise your own meat), and can be placed in a basement or garage.

Where to put your Pantry

But some houses have so little storage space available that it is impossible to have an area dedicated to a pantry, so what is a homemaker to do then? This is where you need to get creative in your thinking. Look around your house for unused space. Quite often there is unused space under a bed, and you can slide a plastic container filled with canned goods, baking items or toilet paper under it.

If you have a closet that isn't entirely full, you can install shelves on one side wall. Perhaps there is unused space in a bathroom cupboard, or a dresser drawer or two.

Look carefully at the items in your kitchen cabinets – are there items that aren't used often (or at all) that you can store somewhere else or give away? In some houses just making that small adjustment can empty an entire kitchen cabinet.

Many people like to use baskets to decorate their homes, and these can be good containers for small items such as spices and toiletries. One of Aunt Sophie's friends built a shelving unit the same height and length as her couch, covered it with a pretty cloth and used it as a sofa table in her living room. Even the smallest house will have some space available!

Organizing your Pantry

Once you have found the place for your pantry you can start stocking it. Aunt Sophie knows how much easier it is for the homemaker if like things are placed together – fruits in one area, vegetables together, baking supplies together, grains together, etc.

One important thing to remember is that whatever food you store can also be food for bugs and mice, so it needs to be protected. Whenever possible don't place items directly on the floor, but place your bottom shelf a few inches up to allow for cleaning under the shelf. Food that comes in cans or jars is already well protected, but anything that comes in a bag or box needs to be put in a container with a tight-fitting lid. If your items are kept in a garage or unfinished basement, look for heavy plastic, glass or metal containers that mice can't chew through (and don't underestimate their chewing power or determination!). Glass jars with tight fitting lids (like canning jars) can be good containers for flour, grains and beans. Bags of flour, sugar, etc. can be kept together in a large plastic bin. Aunt Sophie also places her flour, grains and beans in the freezer for a couple days before storing them to kill any insects or eggs that may be present (the insects lay their eggs on the grain or beans while they are still in the field – it is a natural occurrence).

Another important thing to do is to write the date that you buy each item on the container somewhere with permanent marker. This will allow you to rotate your items, always using the oldest first. It is sad and wasteful to throw food away just because it wasn't used before its expiration date! When you replenish your pantry, be sure to place the newer items behind the older items so that it is easy to find them and they can be used first.

Stocked Pantry Cupboards

Every new home has to stock the cupboards. It can be a while before they are filled and well-stocked. Take the time to buy a few extras of an item any time it is on sale and soon you'll be cooking and find just what you need right there in the pantry!

The pantry has to be replenished on a regular basis and if left unattended will soon be as bare as Mother Hubbard's cupboards! These are very basic items that are found in every well-stocked pantry!

SPICES & SEASONINGS
Parsley Flakes
Thyme
Oregano
Chili Powder
Paprika
Basil
Italian Seasoning
Garlic
Salt
Turmeric
Cloves
Cinnamon
Black Pepper
Nutmeg
Allspice
Seasoning Salt
Sage
Ginger
Curry Powder
Cumin
Garlic Salt

DRY GOODS
Dried Beans
Brown Sugar
Raw Sugar
Confectioner's Sugar
White Sugar
All-Purpose FlourBread
FlourSelf-Rising Flour
Whole Grains
Rice
Pastas

CANNED GOODS
Evaporated Milk
Sweetened Condensed Milk
Assorted Vegetables
Fruits in 100% Juice
Pie Fillings
Soups
Tomato Sauce
Tomato Paste
Diced Tomatoes
Black Olives
Tuna/Salmon/Sardines

BOXED/BAGGED FOOD GOODS
Dry Milk Powder
Breakfast Cereals
Saltine Crackers
Graham Crackers
Snack Crackers
Tea Bags
Baking Powder & Soda
Salt
Yeast
Cornstarch
Cream of Tartar
Raisins
Coffee
Baking Cocoa
Chocolate Chips
Nuts
Pudding Mixes

Minute Tapioca
Oatmeal Flakes
Grits

BOTTLES & JARS
Powdered Coffee Creamer
Mustard & Ketchup
Mayonnaise
Pickles
Green Olives
Pancake Syrup
Salsas & Chutneys
Honey
Soy Sauce
Steak Sauce
Worcestershire Sauce
Hot Pepper Sauce
Salad Dressings
Peanut Butter
Instant Coffee
Molasses
Cooking Oil
Coconut Oil
Olive Oil
Apple Cider Vinegar
White Distilled Vinegar
Vegetable Shortening

Emergency Essentials

Each and every home should be prepared, have set by and in store, a few essentials for the occurrence of an emergency situation. This should be kept in an accessible place and if you have a pantry storage room, it is the ideal place to keep your emergency essential kits. A kit is a collection of items that is assembled for a specific purpose and stored together. In this case, for use in the event of an emergency, such as power outage, fire, severe and hazardous weather and the like. Emergency kits can be simple and need to be contained to a few containers that can be easily toted along with the family if necessary. Have your kit labeled and ready to use at a moments notice. A wise homekeeper will be prepared for times of emergency that are inevitable in life. For supplies that will be useful and can be kept, readily accessible in the pantry, fill 4 proper containers with:

Emergency Essentials
Flashlight
Batteries
Waterproof matches
Candles
Rope
Screwdriver
Small folding shovel
Waterproof ponchos
Can Opener
Small Hammer
Tacks
Strong Tape

Personal Essentials
Bar Soap
Toothbrush
Emergency Blanket
Small Bible
Pencil
Small Paper Notebook
Towel
Envelope of Cash $$
Basic Clothing

WATER
Water is essential and the most important thing. Fill one container with bottled water and rotate it every 3 months for a fresh supply in your container.

Food Essentials
Can Soup
Can Tuna
Hard Candy
Can Beans
Granola Bars
Each year this container needs to be replenished and the items used so as to stay viable and fresh. Adjust contents to suit your family. This is to be just enough to keep from starvation if no other food is available.

Bible Memory Verses for the Family

"She looks well to the ways of her household, and does not eat the bread of idleness." Proverbs 31:27 KJV

"She is not afraid of the snow for her household, for all her household are clothed with scarlet."
Proverbs 31:21 KJV

Go to the ant, O slugggard, observe her ways and be wise, which, having no chief, officer or ruler, prepares her food in the summer and gathers her provision in the harvest.
Proverbs 6:6-8 KJV

The Pantry Throughout the Year

MARCH

Aunt Sophie's pantry year starts in March because it is the time when the shelves and freezer are the emptiest. This is when she cleans her pantry, top to bottom (if you don't have a separate pantry, then clean each of your mini-pantry areas). Take all of the items off each shelf, one at a time. Wash the shelf with warm, soapy water and dry. If you have shelf liner on your shelves, now is a good time to replace it if you wish.

Next, replace the items on the shelves, cleaning and examining each item as you go. Look for dented or swollen cans, discolored home-canned items, or evidence of mice or bugs in dry items. If you find any of these, discard them. As you replace the items on the shelf, be sure to put the newest dates in the back and the oldest in the front. Don't forget to go through the same process in your freezer. This is also the month to start the early crops in your garden, if you have one.

APRIL

This is a good month to look for ham on sale (around Easter) and buy enough for your family for a year. Ham freezes well and can be used for many meals rather than just for Easter dinner! Sliced ham can be used for sandwiches, cubed ham is good in casseroles, and ham slices also make a good supper. Aunt Sophie also makes ham stock from the leftover bones and uses it to flavor many soups and bean dishes.

Another Easter item that is good to stock up on is chocolate. Buy leftover chocolate bunnies and eggs after Easter, break them into small pieces, store in an air-tight jar or freeze, and use them in your baking through the year.

MAY

May starts the gardening year in most areas. If you have never gardened before, this may be the right time to start! Begin small – a small plot only 3 feet wide and 6 feet long can provide a lot of food for your family. If a garden space is impossible, consider containers set outside in a sunny spot. Tomatoes grow well this way.

If you already garden, plan to plant with storage in mind! Plan to can or freeze excess tomatoes, beans, peas, squash, potatoes, carrots, spinach....the list is only limited by your space and your family's tastes.

Watch your stores for special prices on ground beef around Memorial Day, 4th of July and Labor Day. Those are good times to stock up.

JUNE

Whether you have your own garden or not, there are always items your family uses that you don't raise yourself. This is the month to start buying seasonal produce at the farmer's market. Look for strawberries this month, and don't be afraid to ask the vendor for a special price on a larger quantity. Other fruits that may be available in your area this month are blackberries, raspberries and asparagus. This is also a good month for the early vegetables such as peas and spinach.

JULY

This month is the beginning of the home canning season. Again, if you don't have your own garden, go to the farmer's market or the grocery store to buy produce in season at a good price. If you are blessed to have a friend who gardens, offer to trade work for produce. Learn how to can or freeze each vegetable or fruit the way your family likes them.

Meats are quite often on sale for "summer grilling" season. Take advantage of the specials at your grocery store. When storing meats in your freezer, be sure to repackage them in freezer safe wrap, bags or containers. The packaging from the store won't protect the meat from freezer burn during long term storage.

AUGUST

By this month, you may be starting to wonder if you will ever be done freezing and canning. Garden produce is at its peak during August, and you may find yourself doing nothing else with your time other than preparing fruits and vegetables for storage! Depending on your situation, consider moving your canning operation outside. In the old days farmer's wives quite often had a "summer kitchen" to keep from heating up the rest of the house during the summer. Since canned goods remain safe to eat for a couple years, don't hesitate to can enough of a particular item to last for more than one year. If you can enough green beans for two years this summer, then you won't need to can them next year.

This is also the month for "back-to-school" specials at the stores. Look for good prices on paper products and school and office supplies.

SEPTEMBER

In northern regions the canning season is beginning to wind down by this month, but in the south it is still in full swing. Continue to look for specials on produce and the farmer's market and at the store, especially on late season vegetables such as squash and pumpkins. Tomato plants can get a "second wind" as the weather begins to turn cooler, so you can expect to find a lot of excess tomatoes at a good price. This is also the beginning of apple season.

Whether your area is turning to autumn already or not, many stores are ready to clear out their canning supplies. This is a good time to stock up on canning jars and rings if you need more, and definitely the non-reusable canning lids!

OCTOBER

By this month your pantry should start to look like it's bursting at the seams with all the produce you've canned and the supplies you've gathered. Although you may still be able to find produce to can and freeze in your area, in most places the gardening season is over. This is a good month to can soups and stews using the end of the garden veggies. This is also a good month to make applesauce or cider.

NOVEMBER

This is the month when turkeys go on sale in the stores. Aunt Sophie always buys several turkeys while the prices are low and keeps them in the freezer to use throughout the year. Other items that you can find at good prices this month are ham, cranberries, celery, canned soups, canned vegetables, and baking supplies. Canned pumpkin is another item to stock up on this month.

If you've never made stock from poultry, beef or vegetables, then this is the time to learn. There aren't very many things that make a house feel cozier on cold winter days than a stock pot simmering on the stove.

DECEMBER

Once more this is a good month to stock up on items that go on sale for holiday baking.

JANUARY

After-holiday sales can be a wonderful thing for the prudent homemaker. Aunt Sophie always watches for sales on gift wrap, Christmas cards and other items in the week or two after Christmas. Another item to stock up on is candy canes that can be broken into small pieces and used to flavor homemade candy or hot chocolate. Watch for specials on anything your store may have overbought – sometimes a store manager will slash prices on items like sweet potatoes and cranberries to almost nothing just to get rid of the inventory.

FEBRUARY

Evaluate the Pantry:
❖ *Make changes in the inventory list?*
❖ *Storing too much or not enough of items?*
❖ *What items have you forgotten you may need?*
❖ *Are there items you have that you never use?*

Recipes for Storage

Aunt Sophie knows that during the canning season she can really be creative in the way she uses fruits and vegetables. Although she cans many quarts of tomatoes during the summer, not all of them are just canned tomatoes! She also makes tomato sauce, spaghetti sauce, vegetable soups, tomato juice, vegetable juice....the list seems endless, and is only limited by your family's tastes. If you have never canned before, there are several resources available to help you get started. A favorite classic is the "Ball Blue Book".

Here are some favorite recipes from Aunt Sophie and her friends:

Beef Stock

Ingredients:

    About 7 pounds of meaty beef bones - include marrow bones, knuckle bones, ribs/neck bones

    ½ cup vinegar (helps to pull minerals from the bones to make a rich stock)

    2 cups each coarsely chopped onion, carrots, and celery

    1 Tablespoon thyme

    1 teaspoon pepper

    3 Tablespoon dried parsley

Roast the ribs and neck bones in a 350 degree oven until well browned. Meanwhile, place the marrow and knuckle bones in a large non-aluminum stock pot (Aunt Sophie uses a 16 quart size) with enough water to fill your pot to about 2/3 full. Add the vinegar and let stand for 1 hour. Next, add the browned ribs and neck bones, to the pot. Add the vegetables, and then fill the pot with water up to a couple inches from the rim of your pot. Bring the pot to a boil. When it starts boiling you may see a bubbly scum at the top of your pot - skim this off and discard it. Reduce the heat to a simmer and cover. Simmer for at least 12 hours and up to 72 hours. Just before finishing, add the thyme, pepper and parsley and simmer for an additional 10 minutes.

Next you need to remove the bones and strain the stock. Using tongs or a slotted spoon, remove as many of the bones and vegetable pieces as you can. Place a colander over a large bowl and strain the rest of the stock through it in small batches, placing the clear stock in a clean container. Now you are ready to either freeze or can your stock.

If you are going to freeze the stock, you need to cool it first. It is very important that your stock cools within 4 hours for food safety reasons, so handle it carefully. Put the stock into smaller containers and place in your refrigerator. Caution: if you have a large amount of stock you can raise the temperature in your refrigerator dangerously high, so the refrigerator only works well for smaller quantities. If the weather is cold you can cool the stock (again in smaller containers so that it cools quickly) in an unheated garage or outside. Once the stock is cool you can skim the congealed fat off the top, then ladle it into freezer containers, label the containers and place them in your freezer.

You can also can your stock. Prepare your jars, either quarts or pints, and fill with hot stock. Fill only enough jars to fill your canner once, and keep the rest of the stock simmering on the stove until you're ready to can it. Always can meat products in a pressure canner, following the manufacturer's instructions. Let the jars cool, label them, and store them until you are ready to use them. As they cool, fat will gather at the top of the jar and solidify. It is easily removed when you open the jar to use the stock.

Poultry Stock

Ingredients: 1 whole chicken or a turkey carcass with some meat still on it

4 quarts water

2 Tablespoon vinegar

3 cups coarsely chopped vegetables: onion, carrots and celery

2 Tablespoon dried parsley

Cut the chicken or turkey into several pieces, place in a large non-aluminum stock pot and cover with water. Add more water to cover, if necessary. Add the vinegar and vegetables, and let sit for 30 minutes to an hour. Bring to a boil, and remove any scum that may rise to the top. Reduce heat, cover, and let simmer for 6 or up to 24 hours. The longer you simmer the stock, the richer it will be. Add the parsley to the stock about 10 minutes before finishing.

Remove the bones, strain the stock and can or freeze as with beef stock. The leftover meat can be used in soups or casseroles. You can also make ham stock the same way, using a leftover ham bone.

Vegetable Stock

Gather a variety of vegetable scraps and pieces - radish leaves, carrots tops, sliced carrots, green onions, turnip greens, spinach, celery, etc. until you have about 6 to 8 cups. Add a couple onions, quartered. Place vegetables in a large pot and add 8 quarts water. Bring to a boil, reduce heat, cover and simmer for 2 to 4 hours. Strain the broth, then can or freeze.

Vegetable Powder

Aunt Sophie's friend, Aunt Patsy, tells how she uses her vegetable leftovers:

Each year during harvest time I start a vegetable powder jar. I use all the small amounts of vegetables which are left over when preserving from our garden, dry them, and grind them up into a powder. Throughout the summer I dump all the different ground up vegetables into my vegetable powder jar and add this mixture to vegetable soups when canning them and to pot pies when preparing them. This vegetable powder adds something to both items that just can't be replicated in the store.

Beans

One of the easiest kinds of foods to store is dried beans, and a prudent homemaker plans a menu around them at least once a week. They are an inexpensive and healthy source of protein for your family. Before you can use dried beans, though, they need to be soaked. You need to start preparing a bean dish the day before you want to serve it. Around 12 hours before you want to start cooking the beans (around suppertime the night before) set the beans to soak. Measure out the amount of beans you will be using and wash them in cold water. While you are washing them examine the beans carefully and remove and small stones or discolored beans. Then place the beans in a large bowl and cover with water - use plenty of water because the beans will absorb some while they are soaking. Add 2 Tablespoons of vinegar to the water to help remove the "gassy" effect of the beans. Cover and let soak at room temperature overnight. The next morning drain the beans and rinse them. Now they are ready to be used in your recipe. Beans are good in casseroles, soups or on their own as baked beans.

There is not much pleasure in having stored food if you don't have the
resources to use them. Make a point of planning the menu around
the foods kept in storage. Remember! A wise homemaker
"Stores what she uses and uses what she stores"

Genuine Hospitality

A Guide for Practicing the Art of Hospitality

My dear girls ~

Hospitality is not only a homemaking art to be cultivated, but it is also part of what defines a Christian home. The sweet spirit that fills our homes provides a quiet blessing for those who visit, extending God's grace to all who come within our doors.

But please do not confuse hospitality with "entertaining"! Hospitality gives of what we have, entertaining displays our possessions. Hospitality seeks to serve others, entertaining seeks to impress them. Hospitality flows from an open heart, entertaining is carefully crafted to control what our guests experience.

Practicing hospitality takes time and sacrifice, but it will bless your home and family immeasurably. My prayer is that all of my girls will learn to be lovers of hospitality.

- Aunt Sophie

Hospitality
Home Skills Checklist

*"It is well for you to notice the way your mother does,
and learn the reason she has for her method."*

I can confidently practice genuine hospitality in my home having cultivated an open heart and have:

___ Completed my Hospitality Bible verses

___ Started my own Hospitality Menu collection

___ Invited friends over to our house to share a meal

___ Planned a place for overnight guests to stay

___ Prepared a basket of guest toiletries

___ Planned a get-together for a special occasion

NAME: _____

has passed the requirements in our home listed above and has proven herself a lover of hospitality.

Signed:

MotherDear

"All children are deeply interested in the preparations for company, and in the getting ready every mother will find good opportunity to teach her little daughter many valuable lessons. There is so much to be thought of at this time and so much to be done that the wise woman will take the child into consultation, and by freely discussing plans get help and at the same time train her into the right way to prepare for guests."

from <u>Housekeeping, Cookery, Sewing for Little Girls</u> by Olive Hyde Foster circa ❖ 1922

What Does the Bible Say about Hospitality?

Aunt Sophie always uses the Bible as her guide in everything she does. Here are some of her favorite verses about hospitality. Copy the verses from your own Bible in the space below, and be sure to add your own thoughts on what you learn from each one.

Romans 12:13

_____

_____

_____

_____

_____

_____

I Timothy 3:2

_____

_____

_____

_____

_____

_____

I Peter 4:9

_____

_____

_____

_____

_____

_____

Menus, Meals and Guests

When we invite people into our homes, the first thing we usually think about is what we should serve to eat. Why is this? It's because meal time is fellowship time. It seems to come naturally to us to converse freely while we sit around a table, face to face with those we love and enjoying a good meal. One thing Aunt Sophie does is prepare special menus to serve when guests are invited. By having a menu and shopping list already written out much of the stress is taken out of sharing her home. The menus don't need to be elaborate, and certainly not expensive, but they should consist of good wholesome foods that would please most people.

Don't forget to take the time involved in making each item into consideration when planning your menus. It does not show good hospitality when your guests feel like they are imposing or making a lot of work for the homemaker! Aunt Sophie tries to make her work invisible to her guests. Having simple items that can be prepared ahead of time (like a casserole) or can be prepared quickly while talking to the guests (such as tossing a salad or cooking on an outdoor grill) lets the homemaker concentrate on her guests rather than the meal.

It is also helpful to have two or three menus for each meal. There will be times when you have a family over to your home for the second or third time, or there may be times when you need to adjust a menu for your guests' tastes. Aunt Sophie has learned to tell her guests what she plans to serve when she invites them, and at the same time she asks if there are any allergies or dietary restrictions she should know about. If she learns that what she has planned won't suit she can easily make substitutions.

The wise homemaker also plans clean up time so that she is available to spend time with her guests. The table can be cleared quickly, the plates scraped and stacked or put in the dishwasher, and the leftover food put away in a matter of minutes. The children of the family can help, or if they're able they can do the clearing up on their own.

Empty dishwasher:

You may wonder why this task is the first on the list! Well, the last thing Aunt Sophie does in the kitchen is to start the dishwasher with the dirty dishes in it. Then the dishes are clean and ready to put away first thing in the morning. If your kitchen doesn't have a dishwasher, then skip this step.

Preparation & plans for the main meal of the day:

If you have kept up with Aunt Sophie's checklists, you wrote a menu for this week during your weekly chores last week, and you should have all of the ingredients for your meals available to use. Look at your menu for the day after tomorrow. Is there anything you need to remove from the freezer so it can thaw in the refrigerator? Look at your menu for tomorrow. Is there anything you need to prepare ahead of time? Do you have all the ingredients you need on hand? Now look at your menu for today's main meal. If meat needed to be thawed, it should be in your refrigerator now. Check your recipe, and see how long it will take you to make this meal. Is it a crock pot meal? Then  go ahead and start it now. Otherwise, make a note of what time today you need to start cooking or baking. If you make preparations early on in the day it will make the day run so much smoother.

The rest of Aunt Sophie's daily tasks are done after the evening meal.

Wash dishes:

Even though she has a dish washer, there are always some dishes that Aunt Sophie washes by hand in the sink. Since there are very few of them, this is usually a quick task. If your home is not equipped with this convenient appliance, the dishes can pile up quickly. So take time through the day to keep them washed up. Washing up dishes you use while you are cooking and baking, makes clean up time later, much faster. Keeping dirty dishes rinsed and organized, instead of piled and jumbled in the sink, is a good habit to form.

Sample Guest Menus

*Here are some sample menus for different types of meals – you can make
your own menus using your family's favorite foods.*

Breakfast:

Muffins
Assorted Yogurts
Fruit Mixture (seasonal) Tea ♥ Coffee

Brunch:

Breakfast Casserole
Hash Brown Potatoes
Bacon and Sausage
Coffee
Cake
Juice ♥ Tea and Coffee

Lunch:

Sandwiches [cold meat and cheese laid out on a serving plate, lettuce and condiments]
Soup – Vegetable or Chicken Noodle
Chips ♥ Pretzels ♥ Carrot & Celery Sticks
Cupcakes
Milk ♥ Water

Take It:

[If your guests will be away you can pack lunch for them in a cooler]
Sandwiches
Carrot & Celery Sticks
Home-baked Cookies
Pre-packaged Drinks

Supper:

Lasagna
Tossed Green Salad ♥ Garlic Bread
Ice Cream

Tea 'n' Snacks:

[for your guests who aren't staying for a meal]
Crackers
Cheese, cut into bite size pieces
Vegetable Dip
Carrot and Celery Sticks
Brownies
Tea ♥ Juice ♥ Water

The Attitude of Hospitality

What makes the difference between a home where guests feel welcome and a home where guests feel like a bother? It is the attitude of the homemaker that makes all the difference. Aunt Sophie has developed a list of six virtues for the wise homemaker to cultivate in order to be a godly hostess.

Humility ~

Humility says "my life for yours". A humble homemaker is willing to give of herself, her time and her home so that others feel welcome and loved. A humble homemaker always remembers that it is not her work and efforts that are important, but the Spirit of God showing through her to those she welcomes into her home.

Cleanliness ~

A home that is clean and orderly is a comfortable and relaxing place to be, and a wise homemaker who is able to maintain the cleanliness of her home with ease is not anxious about having guests visit. Effortless maintenance springs from order in the home.

Service ~

This goes hand in hand with humility. A servant anticipates needs, provides comfort and food, and doesn't demand anything from those she is serving.

Generosity ~

A stingy homemaker is no one's friend. Be confident that God has provided what you need and share with an open hand.

Gratitude ~

Be thankful for the home God has given you. Never compare it to your neighbor's house, and never apologize for the shortcomings you may see. Your guests will remember your attitude and the sweet spirit of your home far longer than they will remember the color of your sofa.

Focus ~
Remember that only two things live forever - God's word and people. Keep your focus on those things, and the rest will seem unimportant.

Special Days

*Make some days in life full of folic and fun. Celebrate the day even if there is not a traditional holiday. Invite some friends over and show hospitality. Special days and special occasions are perfect times to practice your skills in hospitality. It can be great fun to plan to celebrate a special day by inviting someone to your home. Revel in your friendships; enjoy the fellowship. God gave us the gift of food and it is always enjoyed when we have someone to share it with us. With permission from MotherDear plan a special day and celebrate. Here is an idea from excerpted from **"Marmee's Kitchen Primer"** to inspire you. Use your worksheets to help you prepare for your own special day.*

SPECIAL DAY PLANNER:

What occasion will we celebrate?
A Hobo Party

Who will be invited and how many?
The Browns & the Petersons + our family = 14 people

When will we have this party?
Saturday, October 9

What time will we begin and end?
Start at 4:00 pm and end at 9:00 pm.

Where will we meet? Which rooms will we use?
We will have a bonfire in the backyard and will eat sitting round the fire after preparing the plates buffet style at the kitchen island.

What food will be served?
Our menu will be sloppy joes, baked oven fries, corn on the cob and chocolate dipsy doodads. Food for after supper snacking during fellowship are homemade cracker jack popcorn mix, and marshmallows for roasting.

What will we drink?
Water.

What plates, cups, tableware and napkins will we use?
We will use disposable tin pie plates, bandanas for napkins, and mason jars for drinking glasses.

How will we decorate the house?
The house will be tidy and clean, bathrooms ready for guests, and the table for the buffet set with red gingham table runner and metal pails of snack items. The bandanas (used for napkins) will be folded and tied up with jute string and everyone can tuck them

in their pocket when going thru the food line and then take the bandana home as a party favor. Oil lamps or tin pails filled with sand and candles will decorate the porch and walkway.

What activities will we do, or what games will we play?
*Everyone will be told to come dressed in old overalls, jean skirts, flannel shirts and straw hats and or old hats. When everyone arrives older ones are going to paint faces with freckles using brown eyeliner. We will eat and have harmonicas and singing around the bonfire and roast marshmallows.

What will each family member do to help?
*Older girls and Mom will make sure all the food is prepared in plenty of time. Sloppy Joes will stay warm in the crock pot. Older boys and Dad will prepare the back yard with chairs and bonfires. Younger children will be passing out marshmallows to all for roasting. Mom and Dad will be the host and hostess at the buffet table. Older boys and girls will clean up after the guests are gone. Dad will make sure bonfire is safely extinguished.

Bonfire—Song Time
Round 1: [Sing loud in rough voice]
There was a HOBO who had a dog and BINGO was his name-O.
B-I-N-G-O B-I-N-G-O B-I-N-G-O and BINGO was his name-O
Round 2: [Sing soft in high voice]
There was a HOBO who had a cat and PINGO was his name-O.
P-I-N-G-O P-I-N-G-O P-I-N-G-O and PINGO was his name-O.
Round 3: [Sing in squeaky voice]There was a HOBO who had a mouse and EEEKO was his name-O.E-E-E-K-O E-E-E-K-O E-E-E-K-O and EEEKO was his name-O.

Planner Worksheet

♥ What occasion will we celebrate?

♥ Who will be invited and how many?

♥ When will we have this party?

♥ What time will we begin and end?

♥ Where will we meet? Which rooms will we use?

♥ What food will be served?

♥ What will we drink?

♥ What plates, cups and napkins will we use?

♥ How will we decorate the house?

♥ What activities will we do, or what games will we play?

♥ What will each family member do to help?

Hospitality in Practice

Aunt Sophie enjoys having family and friends stay with her when they are visiting her area, and she is also thankful that she is able to provide a place for people she hasn't met yet. Some people who have enjoyed Aunt Sophie's hospitality have been guest speakers at her church, missionaries who are on furlough, young people from traveling choirs and youth groups... the list of guests that God brings to her home is endless.

The reason why Aunt Sophie is able to open her home is that she has prepared a place for guests to stay. The example she uses is the story of the woman in the Bible who prepared a place for the prophet Elisha to stay whenever he passed by her home (you can read the story in 2 Kings, chapter 4). Like Aunt Sophie, you can prayerfully ask God to help you prepare a place for the people He brings to your family.

The first thing to consider when preparing a place for your guests is where they will sleep.

If you have an extra bedroom that can become a dedicated guest room, then that is ideal.

This room could double as a sewing room or study, but its primary purpose should be for the guests. It should be furnished with a comfortable bed, a table, a place to set suitcases (possibly the top of a low chest), empty hangers in the closet and a chair or two. Placing a small fan in the room can also add to you guests' comfort. The moving air and quiet noise it provides can help your guests sleep better. A final touch to the room can be a vase of flowers on the table to make your guests feel welcome.

If you don't have an extra room for guests, then think carefully of a space that can be turned into a comfortable and private guest room when needed. One possibility is to have a large bed in one of the children's rooms, and then that room can be converted into a guest room very easily. Another possibility is a family room or den that can be turned into a private room by installing doors that close.

Try to locate the guest room near a bathroom. If you have more than one bathroom, perhaps this one could be given over completely for your guests' use while they are with you. Supply the bathroom with extra tissues, toilet paper and towels – be sure to tell your guests which towels are for their use – and provide a space for them to put their personal toiletries. Sometimes you may have guests who have forgotten certain items. Aunt Sophie buys travel or sample size shampoos, soaps, deodorants and toothpastes, along with extra toothbrushes, and has them available in a pretty basket in the bathroom for her guests.

Considering Your Guests

If you have guests staying with you for an extended time (more than overnight), you will want to be aware of what they will want to do while visiting. If they are people you know well, then their first priority will be to spend time with you. If you live in an area that is known for its tourist attractions, then perhaps your guests will want to spend the days visiting different sights and then spend the evenings with you. Your guests may want to spend time by themselves, or visiting other friends in the area. To be truly hospitable, you will ask your guests what they would like and then abide by their wishes.

Your guests will appreciate it if you provide things to help them pass their time while in your home. A selection of magazines, books, puzzles and games placed where your guests have access to them can give them something to do while relaxing in the evening.

If you live near a tourist destination a selection of brochures can be fun to look through.

If you have television allowed in your home, perhaps your guests have a favorite program that they don't want to miss, (although you should plan on watching your own programs when the rerun shows in a few months!), or maybe they would like to watch one of your videos. The key is to be aware of their desires, and don't be afraid to ask them or make suggestions.

Bible Memory Verses for the Family

"Distributing to the necessity of saints; given to hospitality."
Romans 12:13 KJV

"A bishop then must be blameless, the husband of one wife, vigilant, sober,
Of good behavior, given to hospitality, apt to teach;"
I Timothy 3:2 KJV

"And above all things have fervent charity among yourselves:
for charity shall cover the multitude of sins.
Use hospitality one to another without grudging."
I Peter 4:8 &9 KJV

Advice regarding the "Unexpected Guest" from Grandmother Foster:

"Entertaining can be made easy by some forethought, and a little girl should be made to realize that hospitality in all things, should be genuine. In the case of unexpected company it is well to get whatever is needed in plenty of time, but the unexpected guest should receive none the less cordial greeting while the housekeeper hurriedly reviews her resources in the way of material available. One of the most important lessons to teach the little girl is that of making simple dishes so attractive that no hesitation need be felt in asking friends to share the family fare. This is particularly true in the case of dishes for supper. They should not require much extra work, but be quickly prepared and preferably of what one happens to have in the house. For a light supper it is desirable to have one hot dish, besides a warm bread, cold meat, fruit, cake and tea. If the child has become proficient, she should be allowed as a special favor to make the baking powder biscuits by herself. Have her use a small cutter not more than two inches in diameter, as small biscuits are more appetizing; and be sure to have them baked to light brown."

Comfortable & Tidy Bedrooms

A Guide to Cleaning & Maintaining Bedrooms in the Home

My Dear Girls,

Our bedrooms are unique, personal places. You may have a room to yourself, or you may share your room with a sister (or two, or more), but it is still a place expressly for the use of the people occupying it. Therefore, it is important that you create a space that reflects the people who live in the room.

What is a reflection? A mirror reflects whatever appears before it – a smiling face, a tired face, a bored face, an angry face….which face do you want to present to your family and friends? It is the same with the room that "reflects" your personality. What is it that you want your family and friends to see when they look at your bedroom? Will they see an untidy girl who doesn't care, or an organized young lady who respects herself and her family and seeks to glorify God?

It is up to you to keep your room looking the way you wish for it to look. Think of your bedroom as a practice area for your future home. It may seem like a small thing compared to having the care of an entire home and family, but giving excellent care to your own corner will prepare you for the greater responsibilities to come.

— *Aunt Sophie*

Comfortable & Tidy Bedrooms
Home Skills Checklist

"It is well for you, however, to notice the way your mother does,
and learn the reason she has for her method."
<u>Housekeeping for Little Girls</u> circa ❖ 1922

I can confidently do a good and thorough job knowing the skills needed in the home regarding:

___ How to make a bed
___ How to care for clothing & personal items
___ How to care for a mattress
___ How to clean floors
___ How to dust and care for furniture
___ How to keep a tidy closet
___ Make a pillowcase or dresser scarf

NAME:

_____

has passed the requirements for our home listed above and has proven herself a capable keeper of a home.

Signed:

MotherDear

Grandmother Foster gives instructions to girls:

"On returning from breakfast, first make the bed. Spread the pad on smoothly, and then the lower sheet, placing it with the wide hem always at the top so that the part that touches the feet will come to the bottom every time.

Place the upper sheet on next, with its wide hem at the top, straighten out every wrinkle, and tuck both sheets in well across the bottom. [Nothing is so disagreeable to some people as having the bedclothes pull out at the end.] Then put on the comfort or blankets nice and even, and lastly the spread.

Some housekeepers allow all the covers to hang over the side nearly to the floor—and where there is a valance attached to the mattress-cover as on a brass bed, the clothes can not be tucked in; but if Mother has good old-fashioned wooden bedsteads, then you can fold under everything, leaving a smooth, white inviting bed.

And when the pillows have been well shaken and puffed up as big as possible before laying carefully in place, your bed will look just as it should; then if you have an extra comfort, fold it over and over so as to make a nice roll, and place it across the foot of the bed.

Excerpted from Housekeeping, Cookery, Sewing for Little Girls
by Olive Hyde Foster circa ❖ 1922

Comfortable & Tidy Bedrooms
Home Skills Schedule Chart

DAILY

Air out the room

Make the bed

Take care of clothes

Tidy dresser or other table tops

Put away personal items

MONTHLY

Dust ceilings

Vacuum mattress

Clean under bed

Air or clean blankets
Air pillows
Clean closet

WEEKLY

Dust

Change bed sheets

Clean kitchen window & sill

Vacuum or sweep & mop

SEASONALLY

Wash blankets & mattress pad

Move furniture and vacuum underneath

Clean & organize dresser drawers

Rotate mattress
[Fall=Flip | Spring=Switch]

Clean window treatments & blinds

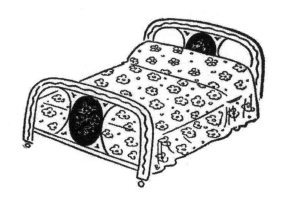

Skills for Daily Cleaning

Just like the other rooms of your home, your bedroom needs daily attention to keep everything neat an orderly. You can do these tasks before you leave your bedroom in the morning, or you can let your bed air until after breakfast. Either way, be sure to finish these chores first thing in the morning!

Air out the room:

If you're getting 8-10 hours of sleep a night, this means that you are spending more than 1/3 of your life in your bedroom! A wise homemaker soon learns that keeping this room fresh and clean is very important to her family's health. Every morning, even in the coldest weather, you can open a window of your room to let fresh air in. In very cold or wet weather, just one window open for an inch for a few minutes will help air out the room without letting the temperature drop too much. In good weather, leave the windows open for as long as possible.

Make your bed:

Making your bed is more than just throwing the covers up over the pillow! A neatly made bed sets the tone for the whole room. If you share your bed with a sister, making the bed can be a team effort and very quickly done.

First throw back the covers and remove the pillows so that you will be able to straighten the sheets underneath. Start with the bottom sheet, smoothing out any wrinkles and re-tucking it under the mattress, if necessary. Next, make sure the top sheet is lying smoothly on top of the mattress, re-tucking the bottom in. Bring the top edge of the sheet right up to the top edge of the mattress.

Now you can start replacing the covers. Lay the blanket on top of the bed, making sure that it lies straight and the edges are even. Line up the top edge of the blanket about three inches below the top edge of the sheet, and fold the sheet edge over the blanket. This helps protect the blanket edge and keeps it clean.

If you have a bedspread or comforter, place it on the bed next. Make sure it is straight and the edges are even all the way around the bed.

Now replace the pillows. If you have a bedspread, fold the top part of the spread back, put the pillows in place, and then bring the top of the spread over the pillows to cover them. If you have decorative pillows in shams or little accent pillows, add them to the head of the bed now.

Take care of your clothing:

I hope that you take care of your clothes as soon as you take them off at night! But in the morning it is time to make sure that any stray socks or blouses are put away or thrown in the laundry hamper. You may wear some items more than once before washing them – don't just throw them over a chair! Find a place in your closet where you can put a hook and hang it there.

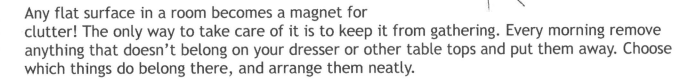

Straighten dresser top and other flat surfaces:

Any flat surface in a room becomes a magnet for clutter! The only way to take care of it is to keep it from gathering. Every morning remove anything that doesn't belong on your dresser or other table tops and put them away. Choose which things do belong there, and arrange them neatly.

Put away personal items:

This task is especially important if you share your room, but it is still necessary even if you have your own room. You may have books, needlework, art supplies or other hobbies that you are working on. These things like to spread out and become a mess! Have a place for everything—and put everything into its own place. Doing this daily will keep the mess from taking over and swallowing up your bedroom!

TIP:
If you don't already have one, ask your mother if you can keep a hamper in your room for laundry. Put all of your soiled clothes into it as you take them off and make it your responsibility to empty your own hamper on laundry day.

Too Much Stuff
by Janet Janzen

There is a little fun song, "Three Blind Mice", you probably learned as a young girl. An ode was written by Janet Janzen [©1990] sung to this cute tune called "Too Much Stuff". If you already know the traditional tune to "Three Blind Mice" you can sing these simple words and remember some good advice!

Too much stuff, Too much stuff,
More than enough, More than enough;
It's out of the closets and filling our space,
It's growing and spilling all over the place,
We're tripping all over a terrible case
of Too much stuff.

Too much stuff, Too much stuff,
More than enough, More than enough;
The piles are staring us in the face,
They multiply at an alarming pace,
And soon we'll be buried without a trace
in Too much stuff.

Too much stuff, Too much stuff,
More than enough, More than enough;
It isn't easy to run the race
With all of this stuff slowing down the pace.
I think that I need some additional grace
for Too much stuff.

Dust Go to Sleep!
By Ruth Hulbert Hamilton

Mother, O Mother, come shake out your cloth,
Empty the dustpan, poison the moth,
Hang out the washing, make up the bed,
Sew on a button and butter the bread.
Where is the mother whose house is so shocking?
She's up in the nursery, blissfully rocking.

Oh, I've grown as shiftless as Little Boy Blue,
Lullabye, rockabye, lullabye loo.
Dishes are waiting and bills are past due,
Lullabye, rockaby, lullabye loo.

The shopping's not done and there's nothing for stew
And out in the yard there's a hullabaloo,
But I'm playing Kanga and this is my Roo,
Lullabye, rockaby lullabye loo.

The cleaning and scrubbing can wait till tomorrow
But children grow up as I've learned to my sorrow.
So quiet down cobwebs;
Dust go to sleep!
I'm rocking my baby and babies don't keep.

Skills for Weekly Cleaning

Choose one day of the week to clean your bedroom. If you share your room, be sure to share the fun of keeping it clean with your sister.

Dust:

Starting at the door of your bedroom, work around the room clockwise, dusting as you go. Use a soft cloth as described in the "Lovely Living Areas" section of this book. Dust everything you come to as you move around the room: door frames, pictures, tables, dressers, bed frames, window sills, etc. Be sure to remove anything that is sitting on your dresser or other tables and dust underneath them. Aunt Sophie also replaces her dresser scarf with a clean one while she dusts.

Change sheets:

Your bed sheets need to be washed regularly just as your clothes do. If your mother has a certain day for washing all of the sheets in the house, then change your sheets on that day, remaking the bed with fresh ones. If washing your own sheets is your responsibility, then ask your mother when the best day would be to use the washing machine.

Vacuum:

Vacuuming or sweeping the floor needs to be done weekly. Vacuum the whole floor, and be sure to use the edge tool to get the area along the floor boards.

You will find, I am sure, that the care of the bedrooms
is one of the most important [as well as one of the most interesting]
parts of all your housekeeping. The sleeping-room can be made
as attractive as any in the house with a little care, just as it can be made
a sight to shut the door on, by neglect.
Not matter how simple the furnishing, it will reflect the charm and personality of its
occupant if always sweet, neat and orderly; and no amount of fine furniture will
overcome the effect on character of dust and disorder.
Therefore—be tidy." - Grandmother Foster

Skills for Monthly Cleaning

Many of the monthly cleaning tasks can be fit in while you're doing your daily or weekly chores, but some will need a special day.

- **Dust Ceilings**
- **Wash Mattress Pad**
- **Vacuum mattress**
- **Clean under Bed**
- **Clean & air blankets and pillows**
- **Clean closet**

Dust Ceilings:
Since Aunt Sophie always cleans a room from top to bottom, she does this chore on the same day that she does her regular weekly dusting and vacuuming.

Take a soft cloth or old towel and fasten it around the bristle end of your broom. Gently sweep along the corners of the room where the walls meet the ceiling and where they meet each other. This will keep cobwebs from being a problem!

Wash mattress pad:
A mattress pad, a thick padding between the bottom sheet and the mattress, also helps to extend the life of your mattress. It doesn't need cleaning as often as your sheets, but it should be laundered once a month.

Vacuum mattress:
While your mattress pad is being washed, use the upholstery attachment of your vacuum cleaner to vacuum the mattress. You would be surprised if you could see how dusty a mattress can get when this isn't done!

Clean under bed:
When all of her children were at home, Aunt Sophie used the space under the beds for much needed storage! But just like any storage areas, that space under the bed needs to be emptied, the items sorted and cleaned, the space vacuumed and the items replaced on a regular basis. Even if you don't use that space for storage, the floor needs to be kept clean. If your vacuum or dust mop doesn't fit under the bed, then you will need to move your bed to clean underneath it. Ask for help to do this - a bed can be heavy!

Air and clean blankets and pillows:

Blankets and pillows are used every day, and once a month they need a bit of freshening up. In the warm months, Aunt Sophie likes to hang them on her clothes line for a few hours. When she brings them back inside they seem to bring fresh air and sunshine in with them! If the weather is bad, then Aunt Sophie puts them in her dryer for a few minutes. The tumbling of the dryer freshens them up.

Cleaning Your Closet:

If you're not careful, your closet can become your worst nightmare. Too many girls use their closet to keep things that they don't know what to do with. As a result, the closet becomes so packed with stuff that there's no place for clothes!

If this describes your closet, then you'll have to schedule an entire day to clean and organize it. But after that marathon organizing day, it will be easy to keep it neat and clean every month.

First of all, decide what you will keep in your closet and how to organize it. Aunt Sophie has found that it is easy to install shelves on one end of the bedroom closets. She uses these shelves to store sweaters and other bulky clothing, shoes, and personal items like her jewelry box. This keeps the rest of her closet from getting too cluttered. Each month, she also sorts through her clothing and gives away anything that she hasn't worn for several months. This keeps the hanging clothes from getting too packed and crowded.

Another thing Aunt Sophie likes to do to keep her closet neat is to organize the clothes on hangars. She hangs all of her dresses together, her blouses together, and her skirts together. It helps keep the closet from looking like a jumbled mess and makes it much easier for her to find her favorite outfit.

Once your closet is organized, monthly cleaning becomes a breeze.

♥ Dust the ceilings in your closet

♥ Straighten the items stored on shelves, dusting the shelves as you go

♥ Remove everything from the floor and vacuum

♥ Replace the items you removed, organizing them neatly

Wheeeeeeeeeeee! You're done!

Skills for Seasonal Cleaning

Because Aunt Sophie knows how important it is to keep her bedrooms fresh and clean, there are very few tasks that aren't done daily, weekly or monthly. By keeping the bedrooms fresh and clean a wise homemaker is contributing to the health of her family. But not all tasks are needed to be accomplished often; here are the few tasks that Aunt Sophie does on a seasonal basis:

Wash Blankets
Vacuum Under All Furniture
Rotate Mattress
Clean Window Treatments
Clean and Organize Dresser Drawers

Wash Blankets:
How you wash your blankets depends on the material they're made from. Most modern blankets can be washed in a large washing machine (ask your mother if your home washing machine will do this task, or if they should be washed in a commercial washer). If you use wool blankets or quilts, extra care needs to be taken to keep these items in good repair. Ask your mother how to wash the blankets your family owns.

Vacuum Under All Furniture:
Dressers, chests, bookshelves, desks, chairs...there can be many types of furniture in a bedroom! The floor underneath the furniture needs to be cleaned every three months. Ask for help to move the furniture, vacuum, and then replace the item. This is a great time to try out a new arrangement for your room!

Rotate mattress:
This is a good task to do during one of the times you're changing the sheets on your bed. If you have a regular mattress, you will want to flip the mattress sometimes, spin it other times. Aunt Sophie <u>flips</u> her mattress in the <u>Fall</u> and <u>spins</u> it in the <u>Spring</u>, [meaning to rotate the mattress so the "foot is at the head"]. This way she can remember which to do next. If you have a "pillow-top" mattress, you will only spin it. Regularly rotating your mattress makes it possible for it to wear evenly, adding years to its life.

MATTRESSES

Clean Window Treatments:

Just like in your living areas, the windows in your bedroom can have a variety of window treatments. Aunt Sophie always says that window treatments should be simple, tasteful and appealing. A simple shade or set of blinds can provide a beautiful backdrop to your room when they are closed, and let plenty of light into the room when they are open. If you have curtains, they should also be simple, in a color or pattern that compliments your room. Your window treatment should be cleaned regularly. Please refer to the "Lovely Living Areas" section of this book for ways to clean different kinds of window coverings.

Clean and Organize Dresser Drawers:

Your dresser drawers should be kept neat and orderly, but just like your closet, it's easy to let them slide by. That's the way it is with any part of your home that isn't seen by other people. Take time to empty each of your drawers, evaluate what you keep in them, and replace the needed items in a neat fashion.

More Helpful Hints from Aunt Sophie

❖ Socks are one item that can quickly get out of hand! To eliminate searching for pairs in your sock drawer, bundle them together when you're folding them after washing them, and then place them neatly in one part of your drawer. An old shoe box works wonderfully to keep socks in their own part of the drawer. You can bundle each pair by rolling them together, or turning the top of each pair over to keep them together. Sort your socks by color to make your drawer look even neater.

❖ If you find that your dresser drawers are too crowded, look for the reason. Do you have too many clothes? Store off-season clothes somewhere else and switch them when the seasons change. If you find that your drawers are still too full, make sure that you actually wear each item that you're storing there. Anything that is out-grown can be passed on. If your drawers are still crowded, look for another storage spot for bulky items. Perhaps sweaters can be stored in a box under your bed, or on a closet shelf.

❖ Aunt Sophie loves to have handmade things around her house. Many of these are little things that she made while she was a girl and making them taught her many valuable skills. As she grew she collected all of the things she had made in a Hope Chest that she took with her to her new home when she married. She has also made embroidered projects for gifts through the years, and many of her friends and relatives have treasured needlework from Aunt Sophie's hands in their own homes.

❖ If you would like to make something special to decorate your bedroom, the perfect thing is to embroider a dresser scarf. If you don't have a dresser, a pillow case for your bed will be just as much fun.

Supplies

To start, you may purchase a "stamped embroidery" project from a sewing or craft store. There are many designs available, and you are sure to find one that fits your taste. Some possible sources are Herschner's, JoAnn Fabrics, Hancock Fabrics or Hobby Lobby. If you don't have a store near you that carries stamped embroidery items, you can purchase them by ordering on-line from any of these stores. Look for designs with pre-finished edges for this project. It is also very simple to just trace with a pencil from a paper pattern, like the designs included here in this section, and then embroider over the penciled lines. Other supplies that you will need are:

An embroidery hoop.
Look for one made of plastic with a screw mechanism that holds the two hoops together. These are easy to use and don't leave marks on your project.

Embroidery needles.
These needles have sharp points and large eyes.

Embroidery floss.
You may find a couple different brands available. It is good to choose one brand of good quality to use for all of your projects. Be sure to look for floss that is "color-fast", which means that the color won't bleed when you wash it. One skein of floss costs less than $.50 and should last through several embroidery pieces. You will need one skein of each color that is required by your project.

Scissors.
You will want sharp scissors, but not large ones. They will only be used for snipping threads. Ask your mother for her advice in finding a pair you can use.

More from Grandmother Foster:

"A closet is a bad place for getting out of order, and unless you are careful every time you put a garment away, will soon appear too crowded to hold any more. Then the remedy is to lay out everything, and replace it the way you like, removing to some other closet [or even a box in the attic] all unnecessary articles. A shelf across the top of the closet will give a lot of extra room for boxes to hold hats, shirtwaists, the party dress, etc., and then there will be space along the under side of the shelf for your father to put in an extra row of hooks so you can hang your clothing two rows deep without creasing or crushing. In your top dresser-drawer you can keep better order too, if you will use separate boxes to hold your handkerchiefs, collars, ties, ribbons, etc. The ribbons, particularly will keep fresh much longer if they are smoothed out each time they are worn and laid out straight or wrapped around a card."

Bedroom Stitching Project

Using Your Embroidery Hoop

To place the embroidery hoop on your fabric, put the smaller ring under the place on your piece where you'll be working. Loosen the screw on the larger ring, and then ease it onto the smaller one with the fabric in between them. Tighten the larger ring, keeping the fabric taut as you do so. When you have finished putting the hoop on, the rings should be secure and the fabric should be taut between them.

Using Embroidery Floss

Embroidery floss for hand embroidery is sold in skeins, held together with two paper bands. The floss itself has six strands. For most embroidery projects you will use three of those strands.

To separate the strands, first cut a length of floss off the skein. You can pull gently on the end of the floss, and it will come out of the skein. The length you cut off should be about 20" long. Cut a shorter length if you are sewing a small amount with that color. Now look at one end of the floss and find the six separate strands. Carefully, with your fingers, untwist three strands from the others. Put the unused strands back with the skein. A small plastic bag can be used to keep them together.

Threading Your Needle

Needle threading is an art that becomes easy with practice! Threading an embroidery needle is extra difficult because you are threading on three strands at once.

Most seamstresses wet the ends of the strands slightly, or you can use a bit of beeswax. This will keep the strands together and give them some stiffness and then you can put the ends of the strands through the eye of the needle.

After threading the needle, you will need to put a knot at the end of your thread. If you make your knot too small it will just pull through your material, but if you make it too large it will make a bump on the back of your piece. Experiment with different size knots for each kind of material you use.

Aunt Sophie likes to use her needle to make easy knots. First, wrap the end of the thread around the needle 3 or 4 times (more wraps make a larger knot). Now pull the needle through the wraps, pulling the thread through also until the wraps tighten at the end of your thread. Try this technique with regular thread several times until you get accustomed to knotting your thread.

Learning Embroidery Stitches

Your pre-stamped material will have the embroidery design imprinted on it. Most designs use only a few basic stitches that you will be able to master easily, and you can practice on a piece of scrap material before starting on your project.

Look at the design you have chosen to determine the stitches you will need. Flower stems and other lines (straight or curved) use the "outline stitch". It you have flowers with petals, you'll be using the "lazy daisy" stitch. If you have small areas that are to be filled with color, you will use the "satin stitch". If there are X's, you'll use the "cross-stitch". To make dots, you use the "French knot". The last common stitch that you may use is the "back stitch", used for lines that aren't suitable for the outline stitch, such as a center line within an outlined leaf.

Outline Stitch:

The outline stitch does just what its name says: it outlines something. Sometimes it is also called the "stem stitch" because it's used for flower and leaf stems. The stitches overlap each other a bit, but not completely. Look closely at the diagram and you will see that your needle should come up at about the half way point on the previous stitch, then go down again about a half-stitch length along your outline. You will feel like you're taking two steps forward and one step back, but this stitch will give you a neat outline.

Lazy Daisy Stitch:

The Lazy Daisy forms flower petals. Using the lines on your project for a guide, make a loop from one end of the "U" shape to the next. Now, without pulling the loop tight, bring your needle up just inside the end of the "U". Take your needle through your loop, and then with your fingers, gently tighten the thread until the loop is the right size. Now bring your needle down again on the other side of the "U", and very close to where you brought your needle up. That will fasten the end of the loop to your fabric.

Satin Stitch:

This is the stitch that is used to fill in sections with color. It's hard to keep this stitch neat and to keep the fabric from puckering, so give yourself plenty of time to practice it. To do the stitch, bring your needle down through the fabric on one edge of your design, covering the printed outline. Bring your needle back up on the other edge of the design, then down again on the first edge. When you are done, the front and back of your fabric will look the same.

Key things to remember:
* **Place your stitches carefully. If you use the threads of the fabric as a guide it's easier to keep the stitches even.**
* **Don't pull too tight - the fabric will pucker.**
* **Don't let the threads hang too loose – you won't have an even look to your stitches.**

Cross Stitch:
This stitch is used extensively in another type of embroidery called "counted cross stitch". When you have X's on your printed design, you will use the cross stitch.

This is a very simple stitch.
Bring your needle up on one leg of the cross and down on the opposite side. Then bring your needle up again on the other leg, and down again to form the X. If you always have the first leg of your crosses going the same direction, your stitches will look neater.

French Knot:
The technique for making the French knot is very similar to the way Aunt Sophie puts a knot at the end of her threads. The trick is making sure the knot is where you want it! Be sure to practice this stitch several times before attempting on your project.

Bring your needle up in the place where you want your knot. Wrap the thread around the needle three times, close to the fabric as shown in the diagram. Put your needle back down through the fabric slightly apart from where you brought it up. Only one strand in the weave of your fabric should be between the spots. Carefully pull the needle and thread through the wraps, using one hand to hold the thread slightly taut until it has all passed through the wraps.

Back Stitch:
The back stitch is very similar to the outline stitch, but is used in different places.
To do this stitch, start by bringing your needle up one stitch length (about 1/8") away from

the end of the line on your design. Bring the needle down at the end of the line, and then up again one stitch length ahead of your last stitch. Start the next stitch by bringing your needle down at the end of the previous stitch. The result should be a series of stitches that don't overlap.

Finishing Your Project:

After you have finished with your embroidery design, it's time to get it ready to use.

First, hand wash your dresser scarf carefully in mild, soapy water and rinse thoroughly. Roll it in a clean towel to get the excess water out of it, and then let it dry flat. Next, iron your project. Put a towel on your ironing board to give the surface more cushion, and iron carefully, using the setting for the fabric used in your project (but don't use steam). As you iron go carefully around any French knots, and try to avoid ironing the stitching itself.

Once your piece is ironed, it's done! Place it in your room and enjoy it!

Bible Memory Verses for the Family

" I will both lay me down in peace, and sleep: for thou, LORD, only makest me dwell in safety."

Psalm 4:8 KJV HOLY BIBLE

"It is vain for you to rise up early, to sit up late, to eat the bread of sorrows: for so he giveth his beloved sleep."
Psalm 127:2 KJV HOLY BIBLE

"When thou liest down, thou shalt not be afraid: yea, thou shalt lie down, and thy sleep shall be sweet."
Proverbs 3:24 KJV HOLY BIBLE

Organized Closets

A Guide to Organizing Your Closets in the Home

My Dear Girls,

Does your mother often have to tell you to put away your things? I hope that you aren't the type of girls who scatter their things around willy-nilly and expect someone else to take care of them! But when it is time to take care of your things – whether those things are clothes, books, shoes or crafting supplies – where do you put them away? This lesson will help you make a place for everything so that you can keep everything in its place!

Taking care of your things is good stewardship. You may have received your things as a gift, or worked hard to earn money to spend on some of your things, but in the end, all things come from God. We don't want to dishonor Him by treating His gifts as if we were ungrateful.

How do we show gratitude? By caring for our things with respect so that they will serve us for a long time, by storing them in an organized way so that they are available when we need them, and by passing them on to others when we no longer need them.

This lesson will help you learn how to find a place for everything and keep everything in its place. That's the best way to care for the things God has blessed you with!

- Aunt Sophie

Organized Closets
Home Skills Checklist

I can confidently do a good and thorough job knowing the skills needed in the home regarding:

___ How to store my clothing.
___ How to store my personal items.
___ How to keep my things in their place.
___ How to organize my clothing.
___ How to organize my personal items.
___ How to clean out a messy closet.
___ Make your own closet storage box. (Instructions included here)

NAME: _____
has passed the requirements for our home listed above and has proven herself a capable keeper of a home.

Signed:

MotherDear

Organizing Closets
Home Skills Scheduling Chart

DAILY

Hang up or fold garments that are out of their place.

Put away personal items.

Put shoes in their place.

WEEKLY

Straighten up shelves.

Put clean laundry away neatly.

Check clothes for things that need mending.

MONTHLY

Clean closet by dusting and then sweeping or vacuuming the floor area.

Tidy or rearrange the shelves.

Work with another family member to straighten the toys and games.

Straighten the crafts and hobbies storage shelves.

SEASONALLY

Plan with MotherDear regarding new outfits you may need for the upcoming season.

Exchange seasonal clothes from your closet to strorage. Clean the clothes coming out of storage.

Check your clothes for worn out and out-grown items.

YEARLY

Empty your closet, clean the walls, shelves and floor, and then put everything back in, sorting as you go.

Make one new item for your Hope Chest.

What's In Your Closet?

The "Comfortable & Tidy Bedrooms" section of this guide tells you how to clean your closet, and Aunt Sophie shared a bit of how to organize this tiny room then, but now we'll go deeper into the clothes closet.

Most clothes closets have these items: clothes on hangers, folded clothes (usually bulky items like sweaters), and shoes. You may store other items in your clothes closet, but we'll concentrate on the clothes for now.

Hang• ers (noun) Frame for hanging Garment—a triangular frame of metal, wood, or plastic over which clothes can be draped for storage or display.

Hanging Clothes:

First of all, make sure that all of your hangers are usable. Hangers can last for a long time, but sometimes they can get broken or bent. Hangers also come in different sizes, and they're made from different materials.

There are specialty hangers made for hanging skirts or trousers, or heavy duty hangers made to hang suit jackets or winter coats. You may find that if you use hangers of the same type that your closet will appear more organized and tidy.

Inspect the hangers and discard any that are broken, bent, or unusable.

Remove any hangers that are too small or too large for your clothes. Is there someone else in your family who could use these sizes? If not, donate them to a thrift store.

If you don't have enough hangers now, ask your mother if there are some in the house that you can use, or ask her permission to buy some more at the store.

Next, sort through your clothes:

Remove any that don't fit. Is there something that is too big? You can store it until you grow into it. Is there something that is too small? Even if it's your favorite outfit, it's time to pass it on to someone who can wear it and get as much enjoyment out of it as you have. If there is something that needs to be mended, put it to the side until you can do that task. If it stays in your closet, you'll never remember to mend it.

Are there any clothes that are just worn out? Save something to wear when you do out door or dirty work, and turn the rest into rags or discard them.

When you replace your clothes in your closet, do it in a pleasing, organized way. There are a couple ways to organize your hanging clothes:

You can hang outfits together, placing Sunday or good clothes at one end and everyday clothes at the other.

You can put different parts of outfits together if you like to mix and match them – blouses together, skirts together, jumpers together, dresses together, etc.

You can arrange things by color – blues together, pinks, whites, yellow, reds, etc. If you order your colors by the color wheel, your closet can have a rainbow look! Arranging things by color also helps you make pleasing choices when putting outfits together.

Folded Clothes:

First, sort through your folded clothes the same way you did with your hanging clothes. Folded clothes do well on a shelf or in a container.

Shelves can be installed above your hanging bar, or at one end of your closet.

Shelf dividers are available that will help keep your folded piles neat and separated.

There are good containers to use that are especially made for closets. You could use an open box, either on a shelf or on the floor of your closet. You could also use a plastic storage bin.

If there is no room in your closet, consider using a flat box that is made to slide under your bed.

Shoes:

Shoes are hard because they are often different sizes and shapes. You may have sandals, gym shoes, hiking boots...the list can be endless!

First of all, make sure the shoes in your closet are shoes you need and that they fit you.

Remove all out of season shoes to another storage place, or store them in a separate box in your closet or under your bed.

Find a way to arrange your shoes neatly. There are special 2-tiered shelves made for shoes, and they hold several pair. A shoe rack serves the same purpose.

There are also shoe bags that fit on the back of your closet door. They usually have more openings than you need for your shoes, so you can store other odd shaped items in them.

Remember, if you throw your shoes together in a jumble on the floor, you risk having them damaged or lost. Make it a habit to always store your shoes neatly and with the pairs together.

Other Items:

Because a girl has so many things, her closet in her bedroom is sometimes asked to hold much more than clothes! In fact, the other things can take over the closet so completely that the clothes are lost. Don't let this happen in your closet – control the clutter!

Empty everything that isn't clothes out of your closet and sort through them just as you did your clothes and shoes.

Make three piles: keep, give away and throw away.

From your "keep" pile, sort out the different types of things.
> Are there games and toys? Could some of these be stored with the family games?
> Are there books? Move them to a bookshelf.
> Magazines? Purchase a container for them so that they aren't in a messy stack.
> Craft supplies? See the section on crafts below.

If you don't have them already, ask your parents if you can install shelves on one end of your closet. Use these shelves to store the things from your keep pile, but be sure to organize your things neatly.

Boxes, baskets or plastic storage bins are wonderful for keeping things together and small pieces from getting lost.

If you use matching containers, your shelves will look neat and pretty.

For inexpensive matching containers, use shoeboxes or any other type of fiberboard or cardboard box that you can find and cover them. You can use a variety of methods that are fairly simple, to come up with matching coverings for any basic sturdy box. You can use hot glue to attach a flat ribbon border on the edges and even a bow for a pretty touch. Boxes can be covered in contact paper-it has a sticky backing, designer duct tape, fabric-using spray fabric adhesive and even just plain or printed heavy wrapping paper. Even if they're different sizes, the matching covering will bring them together.

Toys, Games & Puzzles

Store games and toys that younger members of the family use on the lower shelves and place more advanced ones on the top shelves.

When your family purchases or receives a new toy or game, try to remove one of the old ones (give it away or donate it) so that the shelves don't become too crowded.

Toys, games and puzzles are most fun when they're new to your family.
Ask your mother if your family could do a "share and swap" day. Gather up a few items that your family hasn't played with for a while and swap them with another family. After a month or so, you can exchange them back.

A place for everything, and everything in its place!

Bible Verses for the Family

"Strength and honor are her clothing; and she shall rejoice in time to come." Proverbs 31:25 KJV

" For where your treasure is, there will your heart be also."
Luke 12:34 KJV

"Through wisdom is a house builded; and by understanding it is established: and by knowledge shall all the chambers be filled with all precious and pleasant riches."
Proverbs 24:3&4 KJV

"She stretcheth out her hand to the poor;
yea, she reacheth forth her hands to the needy
she is not afraid of snow for her household:
for all her household are clothed with scarlet."
Proverbs 31:20&21 KJV

Craft Items

Aunt Sophie's grandmother loved doing crafts and handy work. She knew how to do almost any kind of needlework you can imagine! She also enjoyed beadwork, rug making and painting. Needless to say, she had a lot of supplies, scraps, leftovers, craft books and magazines. This lovely woman was blessed to live in a house with a tiny closet under the eaves on the second floor. She lined the closet with pretty wallpaper, installed shelves, and kept all of her craft supplies in there.

As a girl just starting out, you probably don't have enough craft items to fill a closet! But now is the time to start keeping craft items organized.

A plastic storage bin, or perhaps a couple, is perfect for craft items. The plastic is rigid (unlike a bag) and can be stacked with other bins. It also keeps your supplies clean and dry.

If you do several kinds of crafts, consider one large bin to keep smaller containers in. Another container that works well for crafts are shoe boxes!

Clean plastic bags (like zipper-type food storage bags) are perfect for keeping the smaller pieces of a project together.

Before you can store your craft items, you need to organize them. Choose an afternoon where you'll have a few hours of uninterrupted time, gather your storage bins or boxes, find a large surface (like the dining room table or your bed) and get to work!

Gather it all together

Before you start anything, you need to know what you're working with. Find all of your craft projects, supplies, books, magazines and bring them to your work area.

Sorting

Start by sorting the supplies into the types of crafts they are. Make a pile for sewing, knitting and crocheting, embroidery, painting, coloring, etc. While you sort, take out anything that is unusable and discard it. Any thread or piece of yarn that is too short, any scrap of cloth that is too small to make anything out of, and anything that is soiled or stained beyond cleaning should be thrown away.

Organize

Tackle each pile separately.

Put items for each project together into its own storage bag or box.

Put things that aren't being used for a specific project together also.

Be careful not to get sidetracked! It's easy to take "just a few minutes" to work on a favorite craft while the supplies are right there in front of you, but don't do it! Save it to reward yourself when you finish your work.

Store

Put all of your craft projects and supplies together in storage boxes.

If you have a lot of things, use different boxes for the different types of crafts.

Find a place to store your newly organized crafts.

> A shelf in your closet.
> Under your bed.
> The family room storage closet.
> The family storage area in the basement.

Always, always
put your things away in their storage boxes
when you've finished using them!

The Hope Chest

Saving Things for Later

As a girl at home, you may be looking forward to the time when you are the homemaker in a house of your own someday. To prepare for that time, you're learning to clean and organize a home, how to sew and do other needlework, how to cook, and many other skills that you will need.

What will you do with all of the knitting, crochet and sewing projects? Where will you keep the recipes that you master? Where will you store your notebook of homemaking hints?

The answer is a Hope Chest. The Hope Chest is an old tradition with a rich history. What it looks like and what is stored in it varies from girl to girl, but the one thing all Hope Chests have in common is that they contain the dreams of a girl's future.

First, decide what you will use for your Hope Chest.

Your "Hope Chest" can be any type of container that will keep your belongings clean and organized.

The traditional Hope Chest is a wooden box or chest, sometimes made by the girl's father. They are often made of cedar, and always very tasteful and beautiful. These chests become a permanent part of the girl's home from her girlhood through her adult life.

One consideration when choosing a Hope Chest is where it will be kept. Will you keep it in your room? What shape and size will best fit in your room? Perhaps it will fit in a corner of your closet, or you may need to use the space under your bed. If your Hope Chest is to be a traditional, wooden one, perhaps it can do double duty as a seat under your window.

If you aren't able to have a traditional Hope Chest, or if you don't have one yet,   choose a container that is large enough to hold items you want to store in it.

Plastic storage bins work well for a temporary Hope Chest.

A sturdy cardboard box can also be used.

Perhaps your grandparents or another relative has a chest that has been in the family for a long time. These heirlooms from another time are wonderful Hope Chests.

Next, start planning what you will keep in your Hope Chest.

This is the perfect place for any needlework that you make for your future home:

- *Embroidered pillowcases and dresser scarves.*

- *Knitting projects. If you're a beginning knitter, making blankets or hats for your future children can provide you with some quick and easy projects for practice!*

- *Crochet projects.*

- *Place mats, tablecloths or table runners.*

The Hope Chest can also be where you keep your own personal collection of recipes. Use a file box or notebook to store your recipes in your Hope Chest.

Ask your mother and grandmothers, aunts and friends if you can copy the recipes of your favorite dishes.

Practice making new recipes as you find them in magazines and on the internet and save your favorites in your file.

Pictures of your family, poems or stories that you've written, and memories of your childhood that you will want to share with your own husband and children someday.

Special items made for you by your friends. Aunt Sophie and her girlfriends used to make handmade things for each other's homes and exchange them. They became a precious addition to her Hope Chest.

Anything you want to save to use in your future home.

As you fill your Hope Chest in the years between now and when you have your own home and family, you will be storing the dreams and memories of your girlhood. It will become precious to you!

For more information about Hope Chests, see the book
The Hope Chest: A Legacy of Love by Rebekah Wilson.

Closet Divider Tabs

These are helpful on a long hanging rod in your clothes closet to keep things where they are meant to be. They sell them at various specialty shops out of heavy molded plastic but you can make your own as they are quite simple and a useful help in closet organization.

You will need heavy card stock. You could use a variety of colors or just use white. You could even recycle the backs of spiral composition pads or use the cardboard from discarded shoe boxes! If you wanted them sturdier you could cut them from plastic empty milk jugs! Here is your pattern and you can get creative and make them however you like. The idea is to make enough to divide up the long line of hanging clothes on a single rod. In my own personal closet my divider labels are

SKIRTS ■ TOPS ■ SUNDAY & DRESSY COATS ■ SWEATERS ■ DRESSES

You label yours however suits your wardrobe — the idea is to divide up your hanging garments in an organized fashion. Cut from heavy paper, cardboard or thin plastic from the pattern below using sharp scissors. Label with stickers or permanent marker. Label each divider as you like and slip onto the rod to keep the cloths divided and in the right spot! 2 Patterns included. The one with the smaller opening that is shorter fits well on rods with wire shelving that have the small thin rods attached to a shelf above. The larger opening fits well on round hanging poles.

This is where labels are so helpful because everyone in the family can learn where things go and help keep your home running efficiently.

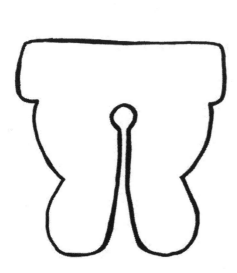 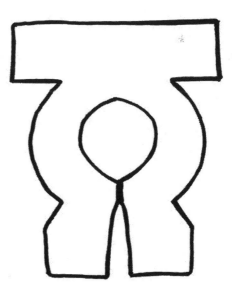

Wire hanging shelf & rod sized divider   Larger pole-sized rod divider

Yards and Porches

A Guide to Caring for Yards & Porches at Home

My Dear Girls -

We have finally come around to the outside of our homes: our yards and porches!

There is nothing that says "Welcome to our Home" like an inviting entryway. A pretty decoration, a colorful plant, a couple of comfortable chairs... all of these invite guests to come in, relax and enjoy a time of refreshing hospitality.

Through the lessons in these sections of the Girl's Guide, I hope that my dear girls have learned how important it is to establish routines to keep your homes clean and organized, but I also hope you have learned a lesson that is far beyond that - our lives,
> and our homes,
>> belong to our Lord Jesus Christ,
>>> and they are meant to be shared.

So share your homes with joy, and may God bless you throughout your lives.

- Aunt Sophie

Yards and Porches
Home Skills Checklist

I can confidently do a good and thorough job taking care of the yard and porch by knowing the skills regarding:

____ How to choose plants for our yard

____ How to clean the porches or entryways

____ How to care for bird feeders and bird baths

____ How to care for plants in containers or pots

____ How to dust and care for furniture

____ How to choose and care for lovely decorations for our porch

____ How to keep the porches clean and tidy

NAME: _____
has passed the requirements for our home listed above and has proven herself a capable keeper of a home.

Signed:

MotherDear

Yards and Porches
Home Skills Scheduling Chart

DAILY

Sweep / shovel the porches and front entryway

Water any plants in containers if needed

Fill bird feeders

Freshen bird bath

WEEKLY

Clean up any debris or falling petals or leaves around plants

Sweep the porch walk and driveway

Sweep away any spider webs

Mow the yard

Take care of weeds

Clean the bird bath

MONTHLY

Fertilize plants, especially potted plants

Freshen any outdoor decorations

Wash any outdoor furniture

SEASONALLY

Change decorations with the seasons

YEARLY

Wash the porches

Look closely and evaluate the yard and porches for necessary fix-ups

Tidy, Inviting Yards

Our front yards and porches are the first things we see when we come home after being away. They should be welcoming and inviting, no matter what the season. They should make us want to be home with our loved ones.

One way to invoke that feeling is to make the entrance to our homes pleasing to the eyes. Flowers and other plantings add softness to our homes and beauty that we can share with our friends and neighbors.

As you choose plants for your front yard, remember that although most plants are purely for decoration, sometimes a blueberry bush or apple tree can make beautiful (and delicious!) addition to your yard. But, oh- - -the variety! Flowers, vines, shrubs, trees...there are so many to choose from!

Planning Your Yard

Before you start planting willy-nilly, stop and make a plan. Draw a map of your front yard and entryway, making sure to mark where existing plants are, and then take a picture of what it looks like now. With your family, decide how you want to use your front yard and entrance.

> *Will it be a play area for children?*
> *Will it be a flower garden?*
> *Is it a good place for fruit trees and shrubs?*
> *Is it an area where you want to attract birds or wildlife?*

If you decide you want a flower garden, think about which colors will go best with your house and do some research to find out which kinds of plants grow best in your growing zone and the amount of sunlight the front of your house has. Decide if some of the existing plants are too old and should be removed or trimmed back. Whether you decide to make changes to your front yard or not, you will still need to maintain what you have so that it has a pleasing appearance.

Birds like food, water and shelter. You can attract many different kinds of birds by placing a bird feeder and bird bath close to a tree or some shrubs, but not so close to the cover that a cat can hide easily and bother the birds.

Skills for Daily Care

Sweep/shovel the porch and front steps:

Every day step out on the front porch and sweep off any dust or leaves that may have wandered up there during the night. In the winter, a quick sweep will dust off newly fallen snow – as long as it's less than two inches deep! More than that will need a shovel.

Water plants in containers:

If you have plants in containers on your porch or along your sidewalk, they will need water every day.

Fill bird feeders:

Keeping a fresh supply of food in your bird feeders is the key to keeping the birds coming every day. They will put your yard on their regular route through your neighborhood.

You don't need to fill the feeders to the top, though. Use a plastic cup or scoop to measure a cup or two a day.

Freshen the bird bath:

Birds need fresh water, too. Every day, dump out the old water and fill it with fresh.

Compost

To help your soil get healthy and stay healthy, you can use homemade compost as both a mulch and a fertilizer. As a fertilizer, dig a few inches of compost into your yard or flower garden beds each fall and spring. To use as a mulch, place generous mounds of compost around established plants. It helps prevent weeds, locks in moisture for the plants and keeps the ground warm. See our KITCHEN section on a bit about "compost".

Outdoor Centerpiece

Fill a large, vintage, galvanized, metal wash pot with richly composted garden soil. Stand an old post from a cedar tree trunk in the middle and tamp soil firmly around the trunk post. Attach a birdhouse to the top of the post. Plant morning glories to grow and allow them to twine around the post as they grow. Plant varieties of mint and chives or other flowering herbs in the wash pot to fill in the area around the base of the post. Plant thickly and allow the plants to cascade over the edges of the tub.

Back Yard Bird Treats

These hang from a tree limb or post in your yard and give the birds a tasty treat. Enjoy watching the feathered friends who come to eat from the treats you set out for them in your own yard! Simple to make!

Use a 1 cup measure and fill it half-full of cold water. Sprinkle in two 1/4 oz. packages of unflavored gelatin powder over the water. Let stand for 5 minutes. In a saucepan heat to simmering 1 3/4 cup water and then add in your gelatin mixture. Stir until all gelatin is dispersed into the water. Now stir in 3 cups of birdseed. Let mixture cool until thickened. While mixture is cooling line an empty small tuna can with aluminum foil. Spray the foil with cooking spray or grease with vegetable shortening. When mixture is cooled press into the foil-lined cans. Use a nail or bamboo skewer to make a hole all the way through the pressed mixture. Place cans in freezer for 2 hours. Remove carefully and peel off the foil. Tie a piece of jute, by threading through the small hole, to hang up your treat for the birds.

Skills for Weekly Care

Clean up after the plants:

Plants are living things and need to be cleaned up after occasionally. Once a week take a look at your flower beds and containers. Remove any spent blooms or yellowed leaves and pick up any debris that has fallen to the ground.

Sweep the porch, walk and driveway:

Once a week take your broom beyond your porch and front steps down the sidewalk and into the driveway.

Sweep away spider webs:

While you have the broom out, look up in the corners of your porch. Aunt Sophie likes to leave active spiders with new webs alone. After all, they do provide a valuable service! But after the web is no longer being used, or if it's too close to the front door, remove it with your broom.

Mow the yard:

During the growing season, it's good to keep the grass in your yard trimmed and neat. This is a good job to share with your brothers and sisters.

Take care of weeds:

Weeds will spring up in the yard and flower beds overnight! Removing them while they are still small is much easier than a once-a-year tug of war with established plants!

Clean the bird bath:

To keep your bird bath clean, pour a bit of vinegar into the water once a week (about ½ cup per gallon of water) and scrub the bowl with a brush. Rinse thoroughly, and then fill with clean water.

Build a Birdhouse

Try your hand with a hammer and saw and make this birdhouse to ornament your backyard. A strip of tin flashing is tacked over the joint of the roof ridge. The miniature birdhouse on the front edge is just ornamental and is made from a small square of wood tacked to the front board of the house. The decorative wood fence is made from small strips of wood or straight twigs and tacked on with small tacks. The house could be painted or left as natural wood. The miniature house on the front shows up best if it contrasts with the color of the house front. An appealing look is a dark green painted birdhouse and a white roof, natural twig fence and red miniature bird house front

Skills for Monthly Care

Fertilize plants, especially containers:

During the growing season, your shrubs and flowers are using up a lot of nutrients from the ground. Feed them regularly with a commercial fertilizer, or by "side dressing" them with compost. *("Side dressing" just means that you take a bit of compost and add it to the soil around the base of the plant.)*

Containers need special care. Remember that the only soil they have is what is in their pots, so it needs to be refreshed regularly.

Freshen decorations:

Decorations look so pretty when we first put them out, but after some wind, dust and rain, they need to be freshened up. Straighten, dust, wash and reset your decorations or maybe they need to be PUT AWAY for another time and another season?

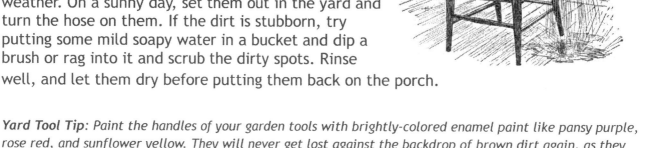

Wash outdoor furniture:

Your outdoor furniture also gets a beating from the weather. On a sunny day, set them out in the yard and turn the hose on them. If the dirt is stubborn, try putting some mild soapy water in a bucket and dip a brush or rag into it and scrub the dirty spots. Rinse well, and let them dry before putting them back on the porch.

Yard Tool Tip: Paint the handles of your garden tools with brightly-colored enamel paint like pansy purple, rose red, and sunflower yellow. They will never get lost against the backdrop of brown dirt again, as they will be easily spotted anywhere in the garden or yard!

Bible Memory Verses for the Family

"I am the door: by me if any man enter in, he shall be saved, and shall go in and out, and find pasture." John 10:9 KJV

" A time to plant, and a time to pluck up that which is planted;"
Ecclesiastes 3:2b KJV

Skills for Seasonal Care

Change decorations with the seasons:

At the beginning of a new season, it's time to put away the old decorations after cleaning them. Store them in a plastic tote or other container that will keep them clean and uncrushed until next year, and then replace them with the decorations you put away last year.

Be sure to look carefully at the decorations you're taking out of storage:

> *Does anything need to be cleaned or repaired?*
> *Does anything need to be replaced?*
> *Watch for after season sales and try to add a new item each year that will be nice to add to your collection.*

Skills for Yearly Care

Take a close look:

Once a year, look at your front yard and entry with your parents and evaluate what you see. Perhaps some paint needs to be touched up or minor repairs need to be done.

Look closely at the furniture and plant containers – do any of them need to be repaired or replaced?

Wash the porches:

The front of your house and the walls under the porch roof can get very dirty, so once a year it's time to wash them. Choose a warm, sunny day for this job! If your home's porches extend around the sides or you also have a back porch this can be a big job! Enlist some willing helpers!

Use a hose, bucket of soapy water and a long-handled scrub brush. Dip the brush in the soapy water and lightly scrub the walls, the soffits (the area under the eaves), and the ceiling of the porch. Rinse well with the hose – but make sure all windows are closed, first!

Home Skills
Master Schedule

Daily, Weekly, Monthly
Seasonal & Yearly Tasks

Daily Tasks

Bathroom:
Check toilet and wipe down lid and rim with disinfectant
Take any soiled towels, or dirty clothes to the laundry area
Wipe sink and countertop surface
Check trashcan

Kitchen:
Empty dishwasher (if applicable)
Preparations or planning for the daily meal
Wash dishes
Wipe off kitchen countertops
Clean kitchen sink
Sweep kitchen floor
Empty garbage can
Replace dish cloth and towels with fresh ones

Living Rooms:
Pick up and put away
Light dusting
Vacuum or sweep floor

Bedrooms:
Air out the room
Make the bed
Take care of clothes
Tidy dresser or other table tops
Put away personal items

Closets:
Hang up or fold garments that are out of their place
Put away personal items
Put shoes in their place

Yards and Porches:
Sweep/shovel the porch and front steps
Water plants in containers
Fill bird feeders
Freshen the bird bath

Weekly Tasks

Bathrooms:
Clean toilet thoroughly
Clean tub and shower
Clean sink and countertop
Clean mirror
Clean toothbrush holder
Sweep and mop floor
Empty trash and replace liner

Kitchen:
Wipe down small appliances (toaster, microwave, etc.)
Remove items from counters and wipe thoroughly, include stovetop
Clean kitchen window and sill
Clean refrigerator: discard leftovers ,wipe down inside, outside and top
Sweep and mop the kitchen floor
Write out menus and shopping list for next week

Living Rooms:
Dust
Vacuum
Water houseplants

Bedrooms:
Dust
Change sheets
Vacuum

Closets:
Straighten up shelves
Put clean laundry away neatly
Check clothes for things that need mending

Yards and Porches:
Clean up after the plants
Sweep the porch, walk and driveway
Sweep away spider webs
Mow the yard
Take care of weeds
Clean the bird bath

Monthly Tasks

Bathrooms:
Clean out bathroom cupboards and tidy up shelves
Dust corners and ceilings
Wipe down cupboard doors and shelves
Wash shower curtain if needed
Clean drains with baking soda and vinegar

Kitchen:
Clean stove range hood and filter
Dust corners and ceilings
Wipe down cupboard doors and shelves
Clean and organize some cupboards and drawers
Clean inside and outside of refrigerator and trash and compost cans

Living Rooms:
Sort through magazine and paper stacks
Dust and polish furniture
Vacuum couch and chair cushions
Clean under area rugs or shake and clean smaller rugs

Bedrooms:
Dust ceilings
Vacuum mattress
Clean under bed
Air or clean blankets
Air pillows
Clean closet

Closets:
Clean closet by dusting and then sweeping or vacuuming the floor area
Tidy or rearrange the shelves
Work with another family member to straighten the toys and games
Straighten the crafts and hobbies storage shelves

Yards and Porches:
Fertilize plants, especially containers
Freshen decorations
Wash outdoor furniture

Seasonal Tasks

Bathrooms:
Restock cupboards with needed toiletries and supplies
Add a pretty new touch to the room or a fresh coat of paint

Kitchen:
Clean windows and wash curtains and blinds
Clean oven, refrigerator and other large appliances (inside and out, under and over!)
Clean light fixtures
Organize and tidy pantry – heavy clean if necessary

Living Rooms:
Wash windows, blinds and curtains
Add and arrange décor to fit the season
Clean and rearrange books and bookshelves

Bedrooms:
Wash blankets and mattress pad
Move furniture and vacuum underneath
Clean and organize dresser drawers
Rotate mattress [Fall=flip | Spring=spin/switch]
Clean window treatments and blinds

Closets:
Plan with MotherDear regarding new outfits you may need for the upcoming season
Exchange seasonal clothes from your closet to storage.
Clean the clothes coming out of storage
Check your clothes for worn out and out-grown items

Yards and Porches:
Change decorations with the season

Yearly Tasks

Living Rooms
Clean upholstered furniture and cushions
Re-pot houseplants
Clean carpeting and floors

Closets:
Empty your closet, clean the walls, shelves and floor, and then put everything
back in, sorting as you go
Make one new item for your Hope Chest

Yards and Porches:
Take a close look at the yard and porch
Wash the porch

"Housework is something you do that no one notices...
unless you don't do it."

Please Visit Us Online ...

and download
Printable Copies of
selected checklists, charts, patterns,
and bonus project pages for use with this book
(your personal use only)

TheHomemakersMentor.com/GirlsGuideExtras

Printed in Great Britain
by Amazon